# Frank
# SINATRA

# Frank SINATRA

Jessica Hodge

CHARTWELL
BOOKS, INC.

This edition published in 1998 by
CHARTWELL BOOKS, INC.
A division of BOOK SALES, INC
114 Northfield Avenue,
Edison, New Jersey 08837

Produced by
PRC Publishing Ltd.,
Kiln House, 210 New Kings Road, London SW6 4NZ

© 1998 PRC Publishing Ltd.

ISBN 0 78580 994 5

Printed and bound in the USA

**Page 1:** Sinatra as the well-to-do boy next door in
*Higher and Higher*, his third film and first major role,
made in 1943.

**Page 2:** The swinging Sinatra continued to make
rapturously received comebacks after his 'retirement'
in 1971.

**Right:** A publicity still released by MGM for *Anchors
Aweigh*, the first film to pair the singing and dancing
talents of Sinatra and Gene Kelly.

**Far right:** Sinatra as he appeared in *Anchors Aweigh*.

# Contents

# Chapter 1
# JOURNEY TO STARDOM
## *1915-1942*

FRANCIS Albert Sinatra was born on December 12, 1915 into an Italian family in the sprawling seaport of Hoboken, New Jersey. Once a resort for New York's wealthy, Hoboken by the turn of the century had been flooded by waves of immigrants in search of the freedom and prosperity the United States promised. The Italians, regarded as the bottom of the heap, settled mainly on the west side of town, a dirty downtown area dominated by concrete foundries and five-story wooden tenements. Many had arrived in their newly adopted country without papers, and immigration officials stamped their immigration cards accordingly, W.O.P.,

*Right:* Sinatra as a young boy with his powerful mother Dolly. The relationship remained a close one despite Dolly's disapproval of the emotional complications in Frank's life, and he was stricken by her death in an airplane crash in 1977.

which rapidly became a term of casual disparagement.

Both the young Francis' parents had come with their families from other urban waterfronts, Natalie Garavanti from Genoa in north Italy and Antony Martin Sinatra from Catania on the east coast of Sicily. Natalie, invariably known from childhood as Dolly because she was considered such a charmer, was a strong-willed gregarious nineteen-year-old when she first began dating Marty, the illiterate son of a boilermaker who had never held a steady job but lived a rough and precarious existence as a boxer. The Garavantis were less than enthusiastic about the relationship, but Dolly borrowed her brothers' clothes – women were not allowed to attend boxing matches then – and crept out of the house every night. Such was the prejudice against Italians that Marty had to fight under the Irish name O'Brien to be allowed into the ring. When Dolly's parents refused her a wedding, she and Marty settled for a City Hall marriage, on February 14, 1914.

Frank was born nearly two years after his parents' marriage, in the apartment they rented. They shared a bathroom and the water was cold but they were already one step ahead of many of their neighbors, with their one-room living and toilet in the yard. The birth was a difficult one. The baby was huge, over thirteen pounds; forceps had to be used, and he emerged with a damaged ear and a bleeding face. Dolly was unable to have more children, and Sinatra carries the visible scars of that birth to this day, having refused at an early stage of his career to have the suggested plastic surgery. The insecurity that continued periodically to surface, and the need to surround himself with unquestioning courtiers, may perhaps be attributed to the emotional trauma of such a difficult passage into the world.

With America's entry into World War I on April 2, 1917, Hoboken became a principal port of embarkation for American troops. Dolly Sinatra used her local contacts as leader of her ward, the first time the position had been held by an immigrant woman, to get her husband work as a boilermaker in the Hoboken shipyards. She herself was made official interpreter to the municipal court, formalizing the role of local spokeswoman that she had already adopted. With the end of the war, American women won the right to vote and Dolly became increasingly involved with the local Democrat Party of New Jersey's Hudson County, a corrupt political machine run by Mayor Frank Hague of Jersey City. All this activity gave Dolly little time for mothering, and the young Francis Albert spent most of his time either with his grandmother Rosa in her local grocery store or with an elderly Jewish neighbor.

Many years later Dolly was to say that she had really wanted a girl: 'I bought a lot of pink clothes when Frank was born. I didn't care. I dressed him in pink anyway. Later I got my mother to make him Little Lord Fauntleroy suits.' Not, perhaps, surprisingly, he was a solitary child, remembered by neighbors and family friends as dawdling about outside his grandmother's house waiting for something to happen. His lack of siblings was unusual in an area more noted for its large dynasties. Sinatra himself said much later: 'In my neighborhood every family had twelve kids and they fought constantly. But whenever there was a beef or a party, you never saw such closeness.' And of course in later years he created and nurtured his own close family circles: the circle of first wife and three children that survived three further marriages and many other liaisons; and the constantly changing but ever-present male support group, the clan, the rat-pack.

At one time Sinatra's publicists liked to portray his childhood as one of grinding hardship and poverty out of which, with super-human determination and talent, the young Frank leaped. Needless to say the story is less simple. Dolly's political activities benefited her family too. There was a bad patch after Marty retired from the ring in 1926, having broken both wrists, and was then laid off from his job as boilermaker because of his asthma, but in August 1927 he was appointed, through Dolly's machinations, to the Hoboken fire department, ultimately rising to the rank of captain. At the same time the family moved out of little Italy into a three-bedroom apartment much closer to the Hudson River. As an only child, Frank's clothes and toys were the envy of his new neighbors; he was nicknamed 'Slacksy' because he had so many pairs of fancy

Left: An awkwardly retouched, undated photograph of the young Frank in one of the formal suits his mother favored.

pants. 'No question about it,' says one contemporary, 'Frank was the richest kid on the block.'

Elementary school was followed by an undistinguished period at David E Rue Junior High. Frank graduated in 1931 into Demarest

High School, where he made himself responsible for hiring musicians for school dances and had his first experience of singing with a band. In the 1920s popular music was live, non-electronic, and by definition smallscale; few entertainers could dominate large theaters or clubs without amplification. But with the first coast-to-coast radio network, NBC, opened in 1927 and swiftly followed by CBS a year later, a national audience was created and vocalists were given a medium in which they could compete with the big bands who had dominated the 1920s, as well as the exposure and the intimate listening conditions denied them in the big dance halls. Gene Austin was the first to sell a million copies of his record 'My Blue Heaven' through this new exposure, but Rudy Vallee took the development one step further by developing a stage personality to complement his singing. He became the first resident host of a network variety show, with his catchcall 'Hey ho everybody.' It was Bing Crosby, however, who inspired the young Frank. He went to all the Crosby movies, started smoking a pipe and wearing Bing's Navy hat. Dolly did not approve; when she saw Crosby's picture in her son's bedroom, she threw a shoe at him and called him a bum.

Accounts vary as to whether Frank was expelled from school, as he later claimed, for 'general rowdiness' or whether he simply left in boredom. He certainly was not a natural student, and yet one contemporary remembers him as wanting a college education desperately – perhaps more for the status it carried than for its own sake. Dolly's son was already developing high ambitions. Singing along with the radio, with friends and family in the evenings, and with various school bands even after his own departure from education, he was convincing himself that his future lay with his voice. Despite her disapproval, his mother funded a portable public address system and orchestrations and, instead of looking for full-time work, the young Sinatra pushed every band he knew to give him work. He would play every local date he could get, for a three or four dollar fee. On top of the orchestrations he bought, he would visit Broadway music publishers trying to blandish them into giving him free music sheets to add to his library. This in turn led to some of his better dates with bands who needed his music and were prepared to give the determined young singer a chance in exchange. The wide variety of gigs and bands was invaluable experience in mastering

*Below:* Frank in 1928, aged thirteen, with his mother.

the technique of voice projection against the big band noise and in drawing audience attention.

The parental gift of a car gave him a further edge. He made himself useful driving local groups, including a trio called The Three Flashes, Italian truck drivers who performed regularly at a local roadhouse. Occasionally he sang with them, but mostly he was just the chauffeur and camp follower. There one night a runner for a radio talent show called Major Bowes' Amateur Hour asked the group to do a couple of film shorts for the program. Needless to say Frank was desperate to be included. Again stories vary: one version has it that at first the group were reluctant to upgrade their driver – until Dolly again pulled local strings. When Major Bowes offered them first an audition and then a spot as contestants on his show, broadcast from the stage of the Capitol Theater in New York City on September 8, 1935, he introduced them as the Hoboken Four. The show was well enough received for

the Major to sign them for one of his traveling units, along with 16 other acts including mouth organists, bell ringers and tap dancers. Two months before his 20th birthday Frank Sinatra was on the road, for $50 a week plus meals.

This, after the initial excitement and novelty had worn off, proved a less than happy experience. Schedules were tight, expenses low, and Sinatra's increasingly obvious confidence in his talent, as well as the cocksure arrogance that that was to continue to get him into trouble all his life, infuriated his co-singers. For some reason wholly baffling to them, their slight unprepossessing lead singer had an extraordinary effect on girls, who would besiege him backstage demanding autographs. From time to time the resulting jealousy boiled over into violence, and they would beat Frank up. He stood both the violence and the tedium for as long as he could, but finally abandoned the dead-end drudgery of amateur touring and returned

*Right:* Major Bowes at the microphone announcing the debut of the Hoboken Four. Frank was only auditioned by the original trio, the Three Flashes, just before they tested for the Major's influential talent show; as Fourth Flash, he made lead singer within a week.

home to the clubs and local radio stations of New Jersey and Manhattan. It was very clear to the already hard-headed young man that the way up was through the radio networks; he gave up his first job back home in Hoboken at the Union Club because it had no radio link, and instead started cajoling the radio offices, just as he had the music publishers, offering to sing for free whenever they had a vacant spot.

Finally in 1938 Frank landed a regular job as singing waiter and master of ceremonies at a smalltime New Jersey roadhouse. The pay was a pitiful $15 a week but the Rustic Cabin had a direct radio line, a wire, to WNEW in New York, and once a week band and singer were heard on the *Saturday Dance Parade*. It was around this time that Sinatra met his manager-to-be, Hank Sanicola, a tough Bronx-bred Italian working as mail clerk at Warners, who helped him acquire the free music sheets that were so essential to staying up-to-date with the new releases.

It was also around this time that Dolly Sinatra was persuaded to abandon her objections to Frank's longterm girlfriend Nancy Barbato. It was with Nancy as early as March 1933 that Frank first heard Bing Crosby sing in a Jersey City vaudeville and determined to be a singer. Nancy had remained loyal throughout the intervening ups and downs and he found an emotional security with her that he had not known before. Dolly's change of heart arouse out of an adultery charge brought by another local girl whom Frank had been seeing – on December 22, 1938 Frank was arrested at the Rustic Cabin and released on $500 bail. Although the charge was eventually dropped, Dolly was alarmed and decided that her susceptible and attractive son would be safer married. Frank was less convinced; he told Nancy that he did not want any woman standing between him and success; 'I dont want anyone dragging on my neck.' 'I'll never get in your way,' replied Nancy, a promise she stalwartly and silently kept.

The marriage took place at the Catholic church of Our Lady of Sorrows in Jersey City on February 4, 1939, and after a four-day honeymoon in North Carolina Frank resumed the round of days hustling up and down Manhattan and nights at the Rustic Cabin. It was here that he learned the casual, confident, intimate banter with the audience that was never to stale through years of night club dates. He did not have the ready wit to match the stand-up comedy routines of Dean Martin or Sammy Davis Jr, but he developed his own inimitable style which was to have audiences eating out of his hand. At this time, too, Frank began to gather round him the first of the support groups which distinguished, and sometimes marred, his career. Hank Sanicola, who now played the piano for Frank on his singing dates, was one member, Nick Sevano, a friend

from Hoboken days, another, and Nancy soon grew resentful of the hours Frank would spend away from home in their company.

The conviction that air time was the key to success paid off that summer of 1939. Harry James, former trumpeter with Benny Goodman's band, had set up his own band some months before and was looking for a vocalist. He had heard Frank on the radio link from the Rustic Cabin and went to see for himself; 'He'd sung only eight bars when I felt the hairs on the back of my neck rising. I knew he was destined to be a great vocalist.' James offered him a two-year contract as the featured male vocalist with his band at $75 a week, and Sinatra was on his way. During the summer months of 1939 the Harry James band played the Roseland Ballroom, Broadway, and *Metronome* magazine gave Frank his first press notice, commending his 'easy vocals.' None of the songs he recorded during five sessions with Harry James made any great impact at the time, but one was to become a Sinatra classic. 'All or Nothing at All' was recorded in August and sold an insignificant 8000 copies; the magazine *Down Beat* remarked that 'the band still has a long way to go.' When the same recording was re-released four years later, it became an instant bestseller.

*Above:* The caption writers of the time called this 'Crooner meets Swooner', as Bing Crosby puts a fatherly arm round the young Sinatra's shoulders. Bing was Frank's teenage idol but by the time this picture was taken in 1943 they were in close competition, as the rather posed atmosphere suggests. They went on to become great friends, however, and starred together in one of Frank's happiest films, *High Society*.

By Christmas the 'skinny little singer' as *Down Beat* condescendingly called him, was impatient for the next move, which turned out to be just round the corner. Jack Leonard, vocalist with top bandleader Tommy Dorsey, was going it alone and Dorsey needed another singer. When offered $125 a week provided he could get out of his contract with James, Sinatra accepted on the spot and to James' eternal credit he made no demur but tore up Sinatra's contract without fuss.

The Dorsey band was the ideal spot for a vocalist; their numbers were usually built round a vocal subject and allowed the singers both musical and stage space. The relationship between Dorsey and his volatile young singer became a formative one. Dorsey knew that he had a star in Sinatra, who in turn adopted the bandleader's flashy way of dressing, his perfectionism, his mannerisms, even his passion for toy trains. That first year was intensely hard work, without the good fun and camaraderie of the months with Harry James. The band was one of the busiest in the country, always filling the gaps between major engagements with one-night gigs on the road. They also took part in Frank's first two full-length films, *Las Vegas Nights* and *Ship Ahoy*, playing themselves. Dorsey was a stern disciplinarian and demanded immense stamina from his team, who might play up to nine 45-minute shows a day, with twelve songs a show. 'No problems,' said Sinatra later, 'No warm-up even. I had real strong pipes in those days.'

As well as discipline and endurance, Sinatra learned from Dorsey the fundamental principles of presentation and showmanship that were to become the hallmarks of his mature years. Dorsey planned the progression from number to number in his shows in detail, with each soloist and vocalist highlighted in turn, and Sinatra showed the same attention to themes and atmosphere in his club dates and records. He learned Dorsey's technique of expressive phrasing, conveying the musical structure as well as the lyrics and mood of a piece while holding the flow of a song without seeming to interrupt it for breath. At first he was baffled by Dorsey's ability to make his trombone sing in long lyrical drawn-out phrases without seeming to breathe; 'He'd stand there playing his trombone and I swear the son of a bitch was not breathing. I couldn't even see his jacket move – nothing.' Perhaps the single most important technical development in Sinatra's singing career was the breathing technique he learned from Dorsey, which enabled him to keep the note sounding while snatching a little extra breath through the side of his mouth.

In other ways too the first year of the new decade was a significant one for Sinatra's burgeoning career. Another member of the Dorsey set-up, who was to play a major role in creating the Sinatra sound, was former trumpeter and vocalist's arranger Axel Stordahl. And on May 23, at Frank's eighth recording session with Dorsey, they cut 'I'll

*Right:* First Lady Eleanor Roosevelt lends her support to a music/sports festival staged in August 1940 to raise funds for a black college in Florida. Tommy Dorsey is on her right, composer Lionel Hampton on her left, and the eager young maestro Sinatra on her far left.

Never Smile Again' – two months later it was top of the hit parade. Although Frank was still an anonymous part of the band's vocals, this first major impact on the record buying public proved to the young singer, if proof he needed, that the big time did not have to be limited to theaters and dance halls. The other high point in a good summer was the birth of Nancy Sandra on June 7 – although her always to be devoted father was, as so often, away from home and was woken with the news in his room at the Astor Hotel, New York.

The constant exposure Frank enjoyed – radio spots, regular disc releases, film appearances – led to growing recognition of his potential as a vocalist in his own right. When the band moved into a vocal number and Sinatra stepped forward, the crowd would gather round. By May 1941 Sinatra had climbed from 22 to top *Billboard*'s annual College Music survey and Victor Records had begun to include his name as a subsidiary credit on Dorsey discs. The adulation he received from female fans proved irresistible, causing the first major rupture in the Sinatra marriage. When Sinatra replaced his idol Bing Crosby at the top of the *Down Beat* poll at the end of 1941, Frank Walker of Victor Records asked Dorsey to let Frank make some solo recordings, which he did in January 1942, with Axel Stordahl as arranger and conductor. He had been itching and clamoring at Dorsey to let him do this for some time, and the accoustics engineer supervising the session was impressed with his self-confidence. 'He came in self-assured, slugging. He knew exactly what he wanted . . . Popularity didn't really change Sinatra. He started out having a good opinion of himself.' He cut four numbers, 'Night and Day,' 'The Night We Called it a Day,' 'The Song is You' and 'Lamplighter's Serenade,' and Axel Stordahl later recalled Sinatra's excitement when he first heard the results; 'I think this was a turning point. I think he began to see what he could do on his own.'

Just the same, it was no easy decision. The only recent vocalist to succeed on his own was Bing Crosby; the pop scene was still largely dominated by live dance music and the big bands. The stress of the decision made him even thinner and more nervy than usual; he lost his appetite and his weight dropped to little more than a hundred pounds. The Dorsey band was a close knit group, and Tommy regarded any defection as a personal affront. During 1942 he altered the programming of his shows to give increasing prominence to his popular young vocalist. As *Variety* recorded in July, 'It is unusual for a band vocalist to get the closing spot in a show. But that's the lot of Frank Sinatra. He fills it – and how!'

The severance from Dorsey was not a gentlemanly business like Frank's departure from the Harry James band. The first of the

rumors linking Sinatra with gangster activites dates from this time. He was already known for his friendships in the tough worlds of boxing and gambling, including allegedly Willie Moretti, *padrino* of New Jersey and certainly a good friend of Sinatra's in later years. The story went that Dorsey refused to negotiate at all until visited persuasively by some Moretti heavies, although both Dorsey and Frank denied that any such event took place. Dorsey certainly negotiated long and hard to hold on to his bright white hope and, even when he recognized defeat, demanded a substantial share in future earnings.

September 1942 was not a good time to go it alone. A musicans' strike had closed recording studios nationwide, and the only immediate work that GAC, Frank's new agents, could find him was a three-minute spot singing 'Night and Day' in a Columbia movie, *Reveille with Beverly*. Manie Sachs of Columbia Records, who became one of Sinatra's firmest supporters in those early difficult days, came to the rescue with a twice weekly radio slot on CBS, *Songs by Sinatra*. This led to a booking at the Mosque Theater in Newark, to which his agent was inspired to bring Bob Weitman, manager of the New York Paramount – he was sufficiently impressed by Sinatra's effect on his audience that he booked him as an extra attraction for Benny Goodman's post-Christmas show a week later.

So it was that on December 30, 1942, paralyzed with stage fright after hearing Benny Goodman dazzle the audience for over an hour, Frank Sinatra walked out onto the stage of the Paramount a brash, green, but determined novice and walked back a star.

*Above:* Sinatra making one of his early solo radio broadcasts in the nervy first days of independence; the stress made him almost impossible to live with.

**Left:** The Voice, the bobbysoxers' dream, pictured in about 1945 wearing his habitual bow tie.

**Right:** Sinatra and Gene Kelly together in *Take Me Out To the Ball Game* (1949).

**Below:** *On the Town* (1949), shot on location in New York, is the story of three sailors looking for fun on 24-hour leave and was greeted with delight by the critics.

**Overleaf:** In *Reveille with Beverly* (1942), Frank played himself, singing the Cole Porter number 'Night and Day.'

# Chapter 2
# THE SWOONING YEARS
# *1943-1946*

THE reception accorded the young Sinatra at the Paramount on December 30, 1942 was unheard of. Benny Goodman, who took little interest in new singers or trends and had never heard of Sinatra, was staggered, and the media were quick to recognize the significance of what had happened. *Life* magazine announced 'the proclamation of a new era;' editorials spoke disapprovingly of mass hypnosis; and the bobbysoxers' reaction was likened to the Children's Crusade. It took

a shrewd publicist to make the most of this instantaneous recognition, and by one of those strokes of good fortune that marked Sinatra's career and seemed to reward his own self-confidence and determination, it was at exactly this point that he acquired one. George Evans, who also handled Glenn Miller, Duke Ellington, Lena Horne, Dean Martin and Jerry Lewis, was recommended by Manie Sachs and came to see Frank in action at the Paramount. It was he who harnessed Sinatra's natural

*Right:* Croon and swoon: Sinatra has just finished singing a love ballad and his enraptured fans at the Paramount burst from listening silence into wild applause. The audience is almost entirely female, and US commentators had seen nothing to equal their reaction to their idol.

ability at the microphone, teaching him to caress it and clutch it as if he were about to collapse with emotion. He also admitted later to paying twelve teenagers to yell, squeal and swoon at the singer's later performances, thus contributing to another Sinatra legend, that of media manipulation. The reaction that Sinatra provoked in his youthful audience was totally unfamiliar to 1940s commentators, some of whom found it hard to believe it genuine. Evans used that reaction to good effect, telling certain selected columnists that the new young singer appearing at the Paramount was going to be bigger than either Bing Crosby or Rudy Vallee because he made women swoon. He may have paid twelve, but when the photographers turned up to record the phenomenon over 30 fainted.

Sinatra's four-week booking with Goodman was extended for another four weeks with lesser known bands, a run only ever exceeded by Crosby and once equalled by Vallee. Evans brought a creative touch to the Sinatra biography, elevating him to a graduate of Demarest High, a sports reporter on *The Jersey Observer*, and a devoted family man, while Dolly became a World War I nurse. The stories of Frank's tough and poverty-stricken childhood also date from this time. In fact the worst povery had been much more recent and Nancy, who had become adept at making a very little go a long way, found it hard to adapt to the freewheeling style her husband adopted even before his success was assured. Evans recognized the tensions in the marriage and was anxious to keep his volatile client out of the gossip columns at this early and sensitive stage in his career. Nick Sevano, Frank's old friend and general factotum, recalled that Evans did everything he could to keep the couple together, lecturing Frank on fidelity, befriending Nancy, and helping to transform her from a shy, though attractive, housewife into a stylish and glamorous woman.

After the sensation at the Paramount the offers and the money rolled in. Sinatra was signed for the weekly networked pop show *Your Hit Parade* for $2800 a week, paid $4500 for a return visit to the Paramount, and $1000 for personal appearances on radio programs such as *The Jack Benny Show*. He also signed a deal with RKO pictures which promised him $25 000 for his first movie, $50 000 for the second and $100 000 for the third. The next move might well have seemed to be a nationwide tour, but Frank had had his fill of touring for a while. Instead he turned his attention to the night club scene – he had the swooners at his feet, now he wanted the socialites. Night clubs were doing big business in early 1943, with civilians earning good money from war contracts and servicemen on leave after a good time, but they were looking for a more upmarket image than the young Sinatra had so

far managed to project. The only club that could be persuaded to give him a spot was the Riobamba, in financial trouble due to late cancellations. Again he was billed as an extra added attraction, and again he was cripplingly nervous, but the club routine was a familiar one from the Rustic Cabin days. Afterwards he said 'I had to open the show walking round the tables and singing . . . I sang a few songs and went off . . . I hadn't really been conscious of any great reception or anything during my act.' But afterwards comic Walter O'Keefe, star of the show, walked on and announced the birth of a new star: one of those classic made-for-the-movies moments. *Variety* hailed 'the hottest thing in show-biz' and Sinatra became standard material for every night club comedian – 'He's so skinny that both of us are trying to get together to do a single,' said one.

When Frank returned to the Paramount in May the critics were there en masse, even from the serious newspapers, to record his reception and their reaction. 'The hysteria which accompanies his act is in no way part of an artistic manifestation,' thundered the *Herald Tribune*; 'Hysteria to the point of swooning is definitely harmful,' warned a psychiatrist. The

*Above:* At a rehearsal for the weekly networked pop program *Your Hit Parade*, the hollow-cheeked young Frank tries out a new dance step. His lean and hungry look inspired helpless devotion in teenage hearts.

head of the New York police department's missing persons bureau blamed Frank for the problem of runaway girls, while the education commissioner charged him with encouraging truancy. Frank became so accustomed to adulation that anything less was bitterly resented and The Varsity, as his entourage were known, began to refer to him behind his back as 'the monster' and Evans as 'Frankenstein.' After one particularly bad screaming session, Frank sacked his old friend and longtime support, Nick Sevano.

There was no stopping the Sinatra juggernaut now. The next bold step was a series of concerts in summer 1943 with four of America's leading symphony orchestras – the Philharmonic, the National of Washington, the Cleveland and the Los Angeles Philharmonic – ostensibly organized to ease the financial problems besetting the large orchestras, but also invaluable publicity. By the time Sinatra went west for the last of his symphony concerts at the Hollywood Bowl and to make the first of his RKO pictures, his reputation had gone before him and he was greeted at Pasadena station by 5000 screaming clawing teenagers. Years later Sinatra said that his

own singing style, originally modeled on Bing Crosby's, had developed into the *bel canto* Italian school of singing and was further influenced by violinist Jascha Heifetz's smooth, sustained, sliding phrasing.

*Higher and Higher* was Sinatra's first starring film role. Although the movie, an improbable story about a household of servants with an elaborate scheme to restore the dismal family fortunes, was damned by David Lardner in *The New Yorker* as 'not particularly engaging,' Sinatra got an honorable mention: 'Mr Sinatra comes out fine. He has some acting to do and he does it.' *The Hollywood Reporter* was more enthusiastic; 'People who have never understood his appeal to swooning fans, have even resented him, will have no trouble in buying the guy they meet on the screen here.' As well as establishing a respectable presence in the film world, Sinatra managed the even more difficult feat of charming the Hollywood gossip machine in a series of well-handled interviews. The *Los Angeles Times* fell for him heavily as 'a romanticist and a dreamer and a careful dresser,' while even the formidable Louella Parsons allowed that he was 'warm, ingenuous, so anxious to please.'

*Below:* When Sinatra went west to make his first RKO movie, *Higher and Higher*, in summer 1943 he tried to avoid the fans by leaving the Santa Fe Chief at Pasadena rather than Los Angeles – but the RKO stepladder suggests that the mob of autograph hunters was not wholly unexpected.

*Above:* Michele Morgan and Sinatra in a still from *Higher and Higher*.

Sinatra was one of the first American popular singers to achieve success as a soloist rather than a big band vocalist but in 1943, his early days as a free agent, the conclusion was anything but foregone. Manie Sachs at Columbia had helped him get his first solo recording breaks the previous autumn with CBS radio, but the major companies were still prevented by a musicians' union recording ban from sign-ing new talent. In May 1943, however, Sachs had the bright idea of re-releasing the old Harry James single 'All or Nothing at All' – within a month it had climbed to the top of the hit parade. Finally in June 1943 Columbia decided to evade the recording ban by using a vocal instead of an instrumental backing, and Manie Sachs was at last authorized to offer Sinatra a recording contract. This was a 16-

21

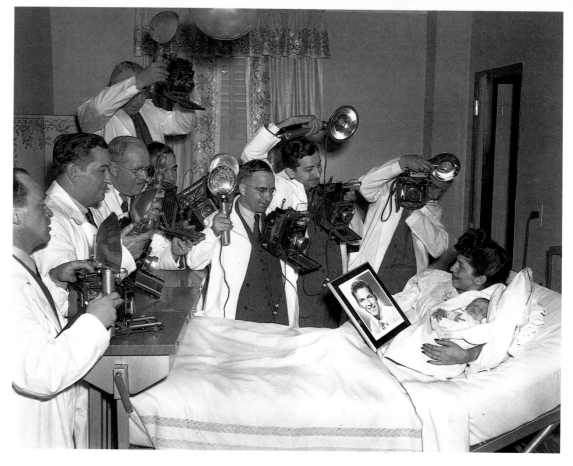

*Right:* Nancy Sinatra, holding the newly born Frank junior in one arm and a photo of Frank senior in the other, is besieged by gowned photographers in her New Jersey maternity home on the day after the birth, January 10, 1944. Frank junior followed his father and older sister Nancy into the world of entertainment, but without the same success.

song agreement for a two-year period, carrying an advance of only $1600, reflecting the crippling effect the recording ban was having on an industry already feeling wartime constraints. A second contract was drawn up well within two years, and a third in 1948 gave Sinatra an advance of $6000 a month, a much more accurate reflection of his drawing power. All three of Sinatra's Columbia releases in the second half of 1943, each with vocal backing, made it to number one.

When Frank junior was born on January 10,

*Right:* In another carefully orchestrated shot, the proud father, filming *Step Lively* in Hollywood, talks to his wife on the telephone while holding a telephoto of her and their new son.

1944, Frank senior was again elsewhere, this time in Hollywood, filming *Step Lively* and starring in a weekly radio show sponsored by Vimms vitamins. When shown the wirephoto of his wife and new-born son, arranged by the ever-efficient George Evans, Frank said 'Fine-looking lad and no bobby socks either.' But he seemed in no hurry to return east. The radio show also starred a number of attractive and glamorous female stars, such as Ginger Rogers, Ann Sheridan and Judy Garland, and it was two and a half months before Frank tore himself away. Meanwhile he and his entourage, including songwriters Sammy Cahn and Jule Styne, who wrote Sinatra's numbers for *Step Lively,* actor Anthony Quinn and old friend Hank Sanicola, formed a softball team called the Swooners. Their supporters included Virginia Mayo, Marilyn Maxwell and Lana Turner.

For a year after Sinatra's first three *a capella* recordings with Columbia the singers observed the musicians' ban and there were no new recordings, except from Decca which had agreed to the royalty demands which lay at the heart of the dispute. This recording silence put an extraordinary premium on live performances by any artist, and above all by Sinatra, who was already way out front in the popularity stakes. One month before the recording ban was finally lifted, in November 1944, he returned to the Paramount Theater, New York, for a three-week engagement of five shows a day. Mayor La Guardia imposed a curfew on juveniles but this was largely ignored. On October 12, Columbus Day, Times Square was jammed by 30 000 teenagers heading for the Paramount and the city of New York went on emergency alert, with reserves called out for the Fifth Avenue Columbus Day parade diverted to deal with what became known as the Columbus Day riot.

Part of Sinatra's appeal lay in the frail, vulnerable image he projected. When London succumbed to the same appeal five years later *The Times* explained: 'To a people whose idea of manhood is husky, full-blooded and self-reliant, he has dared to suggest that under the . . . crashing self-assertion, man is still a child, frightened and whimpering in the dark.' At the same time, however, and in sharp contrast to the light-hearted self-mocking ingenuity of 1920s and 1930s music, Sinatra put feeling and passion back into singing and gave a wartorn generation something to identify with and yearn over. Here was the technique learned

*Below: Step Lively* (1944) was a high spirited musical remake of the Marx Brothers' *Room Service*, in which a team of penniless theatricals bluff out their stay in a hotel until they find a backer for their play. Instead the playwright, naturally played by Sinatra, turns out to have a swoon-worthy voice and takes over the lead in another production, saving the show and winning the girl.

Japanese, and it was the war which caused him his first major publicity upset. Any seemingly fit male who was not in uniform at this time was liable to verbal hassle, and Sinatra's growing fame and continuing success with the bobbysoxers made him more than fair game. In a New York club he had already got himself embroiled in a fight with a couple of Marines who taunted him, – 'Hey, wop, why aren't you in uniform?' – and press comment was also becoming pointed. At Sinatra's preliminary hearing for draft classification he was pronouned 1-A, or fit for active service, but at a second examination in December 1943 he was rejected for service because of a hole in his left eardrum. In February 1945 he was suddenly summoned to report for induction, but was finally classified 2A-F, implying that his normal employment was 'essential to the national health, safety and interest.'

These toings and froings, and the fan hysteria they induced, led to some inevitably cynical press comment. Sinatra's and Evans' response was to organize a tour round the US forces based in Europe and North Africa, which seems to have been well received by those in the field. He toured with comedian Phil Silvers, playing the fall guy to Silvers' bully, and then launching into 'Nancy with the Laughing Face,' written by Silvers with Jimmy van Heusen for little Nancy Sinatra's fourth birthday. On his return Sinatra was extremely critical of the low standard of most of the USO shows and of the 'shoemakers in uniform' who organized them. Press comment was again less than charitable. The New York *Daily Mirror's* columnist Lee Mortimer, later involved in one of the almost routine punch-ups that attended the Sinatra career, wrote that Sinatra 'waited until hostilities were over in the Mediterranean to take his seven-week joy ride, while fragile dolls like Carole Landis and aging, ailing men like Joe E Brown and Al Jolson subjected themselves to enemy action, jungle disease and the dangers of travel through hostile skies from the beginning of the war.'

from Tommy Dorsey in full flow, with long melting phrases, no discernible intake of breath, and each word and phrase extended and given its full potential to charm. As one critic wrote: 'In the larynx of this man these banal phrases become poignant, pointful and even beautiful.' No wonder the doting fans stole his cigarette butts and gathered his footprints in snow to store in their iceboxes.

Sinatra's arrival on screen and radio wave coincided with the beginning of the Allies' territorial campaign against the Germans and

After a brief return home in March 1945, Frank returned to Hollywood to make *Anchors Aweigh* with Gene Kelly, for which Styne wrote the music and Cahn the lyrics. This was a change of studio for Sinatra, from RKO to MGM, and also represents his best performance to date. Louella Parsons judged that it moved him 'right up into the major star class.' Kelly and Sinatra play two sailors on leave in Los Angeles, who get involved with one of those determined and impossible children which Hollywood producers revel in, in this case a small boy who wants to join the navy. A forerunner of *On the Town* in both plot and zestful dance routines, it features Kelly dancing with a cartoon mouse and Sinatra soulfully singing 'I Fall in Love Too Easily.' 'All the

**Right:** Sinatra abandons his singing to address a mixed audience at Benjamin Franklin High School, New York, on the evils of racial prejudice. His anti-racist propaganda short *The House I Live In* dates from the same year, 1945.

world knows Frank Sinatra can sing; now it turns out that he can act too,' said the *Motion Picture Herald*. But Sinatra was already beginning to show a frustration and boredom with the leisurely pace and repetitive nature of filmmaking that was to reappear throughout his acting career. At this point it gave rise to a much-publicized controversy over his reported statement that: 'Pictures stink. Most of the people in them do too. I don't want any more movie acting.' This caused enough of a furore that MGM felt it necessary to draft a mollifying statement.

Frank's next film was a very different production from anything he had done before. In the same year that he made *Anchors Aweigh* he also made *The House I Live In*, directed by Mervyn LeRoy, who had also made *Little Caesar* in 1930, one of the first of a spate of gangster films with a central character clearly based on Al Capone. *The House I Live In* was a ten-minute propaganda short against religious and racial intolerance with a script by Albert Maltz and musical direction by Frank's old ally Axel Stordahl. As an Italian-American Sinatra himself had received his share of abuse, the almost automatic jeers of 'wop' and 'dago', the derogatory conventional view of Italians as simpleminded, volatile and theatrical. And he was never slow to come to the defense of other minority groups. His first recorded public

**Right:** Frank does his bit for the war effort, collecting records, broken and otherwise, at a block dance in Central Park. The reluctant two-year-old is daughter of a Benny Goodman band member.

brawl, in the Dorsey years, was caused by an antisemitic joke at a cocktail party, and at Frank junior's christening in 1944 there was a confrontation when the Roman Catholic priest questioned the nomination of the Jewish Manie Sachs as godfather.

In *The House I Live In* Sinatra is in a rehearsal studio singing 'If You Are But a Dream,' and steps out into an alley for a breath of air during a break. There he sees a group of boys beating up another boy 'because we don't like his religion.' He persuades them that this is no way to behave and, when challenged to prove that he is, as he claims, a singer, sings 'The House I Live In.' Although the film now seems unsubtle to the point of crassness to audiences accustomed to a far more persuasively sophisticated and subliminal approach, it packed a real punch at the time, in a society only just beginning to recognize and question racial discrimination and coming from a well established figure as Sinatra then was. *Cue* hailed its protagonist as ' the bow-tied, fan-eared, scrawny-necked idol of the bobbie-soxers, who has, amazingly, grown within a few short years from a lovelorn microphone-hugging crooner to become one of filmdom's leading and most vocal battlers for a democratic way of life.' The influential and weighty weekly *Time* described the film as 'worthy, heartfelt . . . well-meaning,' and it received a Special Oscar from the Academy of Motion Picture Arts and Sciences.

The Republican press and the Hollywood establishment were less enthusiastic, however; as far as they were concerned this kind of political statement was as unacceptable in a star as bad timekeeping and brawls. His next film, *Till the Clouds Roll By*, a biopic of Jerome Kern in which Frank made a guest appearance singing 'Ole Man River,' also got an extremely mixed reception. *Cue* thought it was 'grand entertainment, not to be missed,' but *Life* suggested that Sinatra in immaculate white tuxedo standing on a white pedestal to sing 'Ole Man River' was the year's worst moment on screen. The cast for *Till the Clouds Roll By* included Judy Garland, long a good friend of Sinatra's and at one time romantically linked with him.

**Right:** Frank all in white singing 'Ole Man River' from *Till the Clouds Roll By*, a scene nominated by *Life* magazine as the year's worst moment on screen.

# Chapter 3
# THE FALL FROM GRACE
## *1946-1952*

THE immediate post-War years seemed to continue the run of success to which Sinatra's career had been building since his decision to become a free agent in 1943. He was America's top night club entertainer, a major film star, and continued to carry off the palm as favorite male singer, winning the *Down Beat* award in 1947 for the third year running. 1946 and 1947 were his busiest recording years, with a total of 123 numbers, including the best-selling 'Coffee Song,' 'Five Minutes More,' 'The Things We Did Last Summer' and 'Full Moon and Empty Arms,' with its theme inspired by Rachmaninov's Second Piano Concerto. His weekly radio show contract was renewed for $12 000 a program and, following the success of *Anchors Aweigh*, he signed a five-year contract with MGM, then the largest movie studio with the greatest number of stars and producing a full-length feature film every

*Right:* Sinatra with Kathryn Grayson, with whom he made several films, and Peter Lawford in *It Happened in Brooklyn* (1947). Sinatra plays returned GI Danny Miller, who at the outset loves only Brooklyn Bridge but by the end has fallen for Gloria Grahame's Brooklyn nurse; 'sheer magic,' said *Cue* magazine.

week. The contract took three months to negotiate and in the end MGM agreed to all Frank's stipulations, including the right to make at least one outside picture a year and the music publishing rights to alternate films.

At the same time, however, these years saw the beginning of a slide. It was hard to see where he could go from here, and there were by now no lack of enemies hoping that the route would be a downward one. Frank arrived on the MGM lot to make *It Happened in Brooklyn* with an all-star cast including Kathryn Grayson – with whom he had already worked in *Anchors Aweigh* – Jimmy Durante, Peter Lawford, who rapidly became a crony, and Gloria Grahame. Unlike most contract players, he arrived as a star in his own right, with his own press agents, entourage and devoted fans, and found the discipline and tedium of movie making increasingly irksome; MGM production memos show that his time-keeping for rehearsals was at best spasmodic, and in September 1946 he left for New York in the middle of shooting to help out old friend Phil Silvers, scheduled to open at the Copabanca Club with a partner, Rags Ragland, who died suddenly two weeks before. They repeated their successful USO routine, with Sinatra as fall guy, and the press reception was ecstatic, both for the routine and for the gesture.

*It Happened in Brooklyn* was well received; 'the big revelation,' according to one reviewer, '. . . is the way Frank Sinatra seems to have loosened up and got into the swing of things as a film player and even a comedian.' And even the critical James Agee allowed that 'Aside from Sinatra and Durante the show amounts to practically nothing, but there is a general kindliness about it which I enjoyed.' Sinatra's songs, written by the usual team of Styne and Cahn, included the classic 'The Song's Gotta Come From the Heart.' The main exception to this generally favorable response was the *New York Daily Mirror*, whose columnist Lee Mortimer had given Sinatra a bad press in the past and who on this occasion wrote that an 'excellent and well-produced picture . . . bogs down under the miscast Frank Sinatra, smirking and trying to play a leading man.'

Sinatra had already rowed with the influential columnist Louella Parsons over stories that he was being unco-operative on the MGM lot. She rebuked him in print and predicted that he could be risking his lucrative MGM contract; his response was a furious telegram – 'I'll appreciate your not wasting your breath in any lectures because when I feel I need one I'll seek such advice from someone who either writes or tells the truth.' Shortly after Mortimer's critical column was published, on April 8, 1947, he and Sinatra were both at Ciro's, a Hollywood nightclub. On his way out, Mortimer had an exchange of words with Sinatra. Needless to

say, versions vary. In some Sinatra followed Mortimer to the door and set on him unprovoked; in others Mortimer began the exchange of insults by referring to Sinatra's alleged relationship with Mafia boss Lucky Luciano. Certainly Mortimer was felled by a Sinatra punch, and in one version he was then held down by Sinatra's friends while the enraged singer continued hitting him.

The background to what seems in retrospect a significant turning point both in Sinatra's relationship with the press and in his overall popularity was a complicated one, connected as much with his political and social standing as with his quick-tempered and heavy-handed response to the slightest provocation. His family background was politically conscious, with his mother's role in local Democrat politics highlighting both the benefits and the downside of patronage. During his early professional years Sinatra was not himself involved in politics or electioneering, but in September 1944 he had been a surprise tea party guest of President Franklin D Roosevelt at the White House. Dolly Sinatra was no supporter of Roosevelt, who had interned 5000 Italian Americans including the opera singer Ezio Pinza, but Frank was charmed and joined

*Above:* A dramatic shot of Sinatra, arraigned on an assault charge in a Beverly Hills Justice Court and firmly ignoring Lee Mortimer's hostile glare. In the end he agreed, under pressure from MGM, to apologize to Mortimer and an out-of-court settlement was reached.

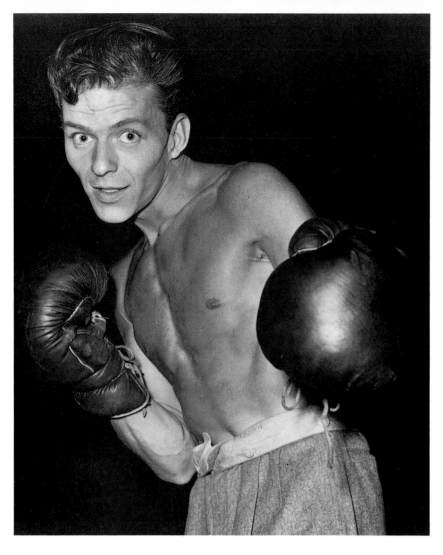

*Above:* Sinatra in suitably pugilistic mood at the time of the assault charge on Mortimer. He was a regular attender at major boxing events and had many cronies in the boxing world.

and gossip-worthy charmers as Lana Turner and Marilyn Maxwell.

In October 1946 radio and press stories reported that the Sinatras had separated. Nancy told press agent George Evans that Frank wanted 'freedom without divorce,' and the errant husband spent three days in Palm Springs, where he was seen dancing with Ava Gardner and dining with Lana Turner. Louella Parsons interviewed Lana, who denied any responsibility, and George Evans confidently predicted a reconciliation. Both he and Manie Sachs of Columbia were worried about the effect of emotional tension on their golden boy – 'It absolutely destroyed him,' according to Evans, 'You could always tell when he was troubled, he came down with a bad throat.' On this occasion a sentimental reunion took place at Phil Silvers' opening night at Slapsie Maxie's in Hollywood. Frank was invited on stage and sang 'Going Home,' and was then led by the faithful Phil to Jule Styne's table, where Nancy sat with her eyes full of tears. For a time the Sinatra household resumed life on a more harmonious note. Frank bought Nancy a full-length ermine coat and a three-strand pearl necklace and took him with her on his trip to New York in November.

More damaging in the popularity stakes than tales of domestic discord were the first openly reported links between Sinatra and friends or acquaintances involved in organized crime. He had first come into contact with the underworld during his early singing days in Hoboken; many of the roadhouses and clubs of New Jersey were under the protection of some local Mafia and Sinatra became friendly with the local *capo*, Willie Moretti, who supposedly sent his heavies to put the frighteners on Tommy Dorsey. As late as 1950, during Frank's well-publicized romance with Ava Gardner that eventually led to the final breakdown of his marriage, Moretti was sending him paternalistic telegrams reminding him that he had a 'decent wife and children.' During the 1930s Sinatra also came to know Joe Fischetti, cousin of Al Capone and member of a solidly Mafia family, who stayed with Frank at the Waldorf-Astoria in New York in summer 1946. In February 1947 the Fischettis and other Mafia bosses gathered in Havana, Cuba, to meet the exiled Mafia leader Charlie 'Lucky' Luciano. Luciano had been instrumental in unifying the various Mafia groups in America after the end of prohibition, forming what later came to be known as the Syndicate or the Organization. He had been jailed on a prohibition charge in 1936 and subsequently deported.

Luciano was being watched by agents of the Federal Narcotics Bureau, and it was they who first reported his meetings with Sinatra. Certainly Sinatra arrived on the same flight as Joe Fischetti, certainly he was photographed

the election campaign. He became a member of the Independent Voters' Committee of the Arts and Sciences for Roosevelt, spoke both at rally meetings and on radio, and contributed $5000 to the election fund. This last gesture made news headlines and antagonized Republican columnists such as Westbrook Pegler, who christened him the 'New Dealing Crooner.' From 1944 on, he got a consistently hostile press from such stalwartly Republican supporters as the Hearst and Scripps-Howard news empires.

There is no doubt, however, that Sinatra gave his enemies plenty of copy. In 1944 he moved his family from their $25 000 suburban New Jersey home to the West Coast, initially to a magnificent residence in the Toluca Lake area once owned by Mary Astor. Instead of being relatively distanced from her husband's flings in Manhattan, Nancy found herself in the center of an intensely inturned gossip-ridden society, all too fascinated by the private lives of the stars. From his earliest successes Frank's fans, in what has since become a time-honored and accepted routine, had adopted their hero's wife and children as part of the legend, and any domestic tension inevitably became newsworthy. Frank found this hard to accept and was infuriated by the publicity that attended his appearances with such noted

dining with Luciano, but Sinatra himself later claimed that the meetings were coincidental. Whatever the truth of the trip to Havana, it led to a new low in Sinatra's public image. A few days after Frank had left to join Nancy in Mexico City for a long-promised vacation, he was denounced by Scripps-Howard columnist Robert Ruark for 'this curious desire to cavort among the scum,' unsuitable in the 'self-confessed savior of the country's small fry,' and for 'setting a most peculiar example for his hordes of pimply, shrieking slaves.' As a result the Cuban police arrested Luciano and then deported him back to Italy, and Frank was widely depicted in the news as being a friend of drug peddlers and mobsters.

Thus when Sinatra socked Mortimer at Ciro's it was the culmination of a long process of mutual provocation between Sinatra and the press, and the whole Hearst organization joined in the fray. Sinatra was arrested during a radio rehearsal and charged with assault and battery. He pleaded not guilty, demanded a jury trial, and was released on bail of $500. Hearst newspapers headlined the incident five days in a row, causing *Time* magazine to comment that this degree of attention was 'almost fit for an attempted political assassination.' The rest of the American press divided fairly equally into those, like Ed Sullivan in the *Daily News*, who felt that Sinatra had acted justifiably given the provocation and those who felt that newspaper commentators should be protected from such possible come-backs. Conviction would have carried a maximum fine of $1000 and/or six months in jail, however, and MGM lawyers were not convinced of the solidity of Frank's case. Under intense

pressure from the MGM head, Louis B Mayer, he was persuaded to settle the affair, expressing regret for the incident and acknowledging that there had been no provocation. Mortimer expressed himself satisfied with this and an out-of-court settlement of $9000, and the charge was withdrawn.

The reverberations continued, however. In the autumn of 1947 Sinatra was scheduled for a three-week season at the Capitol Theater, New York, the first time that he appeared on stage with Sammy Davis Jr, who became one of his closest friends. The New York *Mirror*, a Hearst paper, gave it a bad review, seats remained unfilled and takings were less than half what was expected. An ill-timed change of tack in cinema did not help. In *The Miracle of the Bells*, made with RKO, Sinatra sang only one song in his low-key role as a Catholic priest and the film was poorly received – 'an offensive exhibition of vulgar insensitivity,' thundered one appalled critic. The return to MGM fared no better; *The Kissing Bandit* was at least a musical but, according to *Cue*, 'The frenzied members of Frankie's Fan Clubs are not going to be very happy with their Mr Sinatra's latest picture . . . Never any great shakes as a comic, Mr Sinatra is further handicapped by a weak script, silly dialogue and uncertain direction.' It was an unfair trick of fate that by the time Sinatra made the first of two 1949 films with Gene Kelly, a lively unpretentious comedy musical called *Take Me Out to the Ball Game*, his career was sliding too fast to benefit. Even the gloriously exuberant *On The Town*, the story of three sailors looking for and finding love on 24-hour leave in New York, failed to do him much good. The critics loved it – 'so exuberant,' said *Time magazine*, 'that it threatens at moments to bounce right off the screen' – but Sinatra's role did not rate even a polite mention.

Musically things were going no better. At the end of 1946 Sinatra had abandoned the Cahn-Styne-Stordahl team which had stood him in such good stead and recorded 'Sweet Lorraine' with Sy Oliver and a group of jazz musicians. This suggests an awareness of changing musical fashion, but it was not enough to keep him in the forefront. Pop music was beginning to move away from the lyrical crooning style that made both Crosby and Sinatra toward something harder and more muscular. Frankie Laine and Hank Williams, with his new Nashville sound, appealed more to the bobbysoxers; Perry Como moved in on the crooning, swooning market; and Nat King Cole conquered the clubs which had been Sinatra's particular domain. At the end of 1949 in the *Down Beat* poll, he failed to make number one for the first time since 1943 and managed only fifth place. The arrival of Johnnie Ray on the national music scene in 1950 completed Sinatra's musical eclipse. Like Sinatra before him, Ray mopped up both the teen and the sophisticate market and was to rule pretty well unchallenged until another revolution began six years later when Elvis Presley burst on the scene.

This decline in both his musical and acting careers coincided with yet another traumatic series of events in Sinatra's private life; the love affair with Ava Gardner and the break-up of his marriage to Nancy. The always delicate balance of the Sinatra marriage had seemed to be propped up by the birth of a third child, Christina, in June 1948. But Frank had first met Ava during his brief separation from Nancy in 1946, and in autumn 1948 it seems that the affair took off. The beautiful Ava was a North Carolina girl talent-spotted by an MGM scout and given a seven-year contract in 1941, although at first only with walk-on and supporting roles. She had been married briefly to both Mickey Rooney and bandleader Artie Shaw, each relationship lasting less than a year, and had also been dated by the notoriously womanizing millionaire Howard Hughes.

The Sinatra/Gardner relationship lasted for more than three stormy years. In temperament they were very similar: volatile, hard-drinking, gregarious and possessive. One close friend described the relationship as a 'two-year soap opera with screaming fights heard around the world,' while the London *Daily Sketch* called it ' the most exhausting game of transatlantic ping-pong every played.' At first it was conducted in secret, because in 1948 the scandal caused by an affair with a married man, and one, furthermore, with three children, might have led MGM to drop Ava under the terms of the standard 'morals' clause in her contract. In this the actress agreed to 'conduct herself with

*Above:* From left, Sinatra, Betty Garrett, Jules Munshin, Ann Miller, Gene Kelly and Vera-Ellen finally pair off in *On the Town* (1949), the delightful story of three sailors on 24-hour leave looking for romance. Sinatra was sensitive about his looks and wore pads in the back of his trousers to give his backside a pleasing curve.

due regard for public conventions and morals' and not to do anything that 'will tend to shock, insult or offend the community or ridicule public morals or decency.'

The affair burst on the public scene at the end of 1949, when Frank took Ava to New York and then to Houston for a two-week engagement at the Shamrock Hotel. In February Nancy finally accepted that her marriage was through, hired a lawyer, and announced their separation, although without beginning divorce proceedings. Less than a month earlier, in the same fateful week in January 1950, press agent George Evans, who had tried to remonstrate with Frank about the dangerous path he was treading with Ava, died suddenly of a heart attack at the early age of 47 and Manie Sachs, longterm friend and supporter, resigned from the board of Columbia Records. Thus Sinatra was deprived at a stroke of two of the most stable and sobering influences in his life so far. Press reaction to the Sinatra separation was savage – Frank was depicted as a heel and Ava a home wrecker. When Frank opened at the Copabanca, New York, in March, the emotional and professional tensions were so strong that he needed a sedative and later, as once before when tensions were running high, lost his voice altogether and failed to finish the two-week run. Ava was filming *Pandora and the Flying Dutchman* in Spain and Frank, under doctor's orders to rest, flew over to join her. When filming transferred to London in July

**Above:** Frank escorts the exquisite Ava at the premiere of her smash hit *Show Boat*. They are pictured on a replica of the show boat outside the Egyptian Theater, Hollywood. Although they had been seen in public during the previous eighteen months, this was the first formal occasion on which the pair had appeared together and rumors of a Sinatra divorce were rife.

**Right:** Frank and Ava at the preview of *Meet Danny Wilson* (1951) with Frank's parents. The formidable Dolly took to Ava, preferring her to the more self-effacing Nancy.

the two were again together and had perhaps their happiest two months. But while Ava was pressing for marriage, Nancy was still refusing to consider a divorce, and the granting of her suit for separate maintenance in September left Sinatra strapped for ready money. The cancellation after only 13 weeks of his first television show, for which he signed a three-year contract in autumn 1950, was a disaster – as host on the small screen he could not achieve the fluent relaxed line that had always stood him in good stead on stage, and television remains the one medium where he has never seemed wholly at ease.

In 1951 Sinatra did at last manage to get two film parts. MGM had long since lost interest in their temperamental star, despite the success of *On the Town*, and he moved to RKO to make *Double Dynamite*, and Universal for *Meet Danny Wilson*. The first was a mild comedy, co-starring Groucho Marx and the gorgeous Jane Russell, the second an altogether more abrasive piece in which an overbearing crooner gets to the top with gangster help. Songs included the Gershwin number 'I've Got a Crush on You' and, although the film made no particular impact at the time, Sinatra's acting, admittedly of a tailor-made part, shows a depth and commitment that was new and was finally once more to take him to the top.

In other ways too 1951 was a turning point. The long-postponed marriage to Ava finally took place on November 7, after Nancy gave way and was granted an interlocutory divorce decree. It was a perpetually tempestuous relationship between two demanding, difficult, insecure people, constantly dogged by legendary, glass-shattering rows and enthusiastic but temporary reconciliations. There was little work for Sinatra, while Gardner's stock was soaring high as the star of *Show Boat*. Then Frank read James Jones' bestselling novel *From Here to Eternity*, a tough, no-holds-barred story of life in a Honolulu barracks at the time of Pearl Harbor, and decided that the part of proud, gritty, irrepressible Private Angelo Maggio was for him. He moved heaven and earth to get the part, offering Harry Cohn, head of Columbia Pictures, to do it for far less than his usual fee, a mere $1000 a week. At first the response was cool; Columbia were in negotiation with Eli Wallach for the role and were not interested in a has-been

*Below:* Montgomery Clift, Burt Lancaster and Sinatra, all nominated for Academy Awards for their roles in *From Here to Eternity* (1953).

crooner. But Wallach was holding out for more cash than the picture budget allowed for, and finally Cohn consented to let Sinatra do a screen test. Sinatra flew in from Africa, where he was sitting gloomily around watching Ava make *Mogambo*, did two scenes for his test, and flew straight back to Africa. Director Fred Zinneman was amazed at the quality of the test, particularly a scene where Maggio is found drunk and AWOL, but it was early 1953 before Frank heard that the part of Maggio was his if he would do it for $8000.

The film is, of course, a classic, taking eight Academy Awards, including Best Film, Best Director, and, for Sinatra, Best Supporting Actor. The role of Maggio was a natural for Sinatra but also a total departure from his previous work – only Danny Wilson had shown anything like the range of characterization that he brought to bear. A tough, cocky Italian-American, Maggio grins and boozes his way through army life, befriending Robert E Lee Prewitt (Mongomery Clift) when the latter's refusal to box for his company causes him to be ostracized. Maggio is finally beaten to death by brutal Sergeant Fatso Judson (Ernest Borgnine), dying in Prewitt's arms. He in turn is accidentally killed during the Japanese attack on Pearl Harbor. *From Here to Eternity* is Hollywood in its best, unsentimental form; the film was a roaring hit and established Sinatra as an acting force to be reckoned with. The comeback had begun.

# Chapter 4
# BACK TO THE TOP
## *1953-1960*

WITH *From Here to Eternity* Sinatra was once more on his way, but the climb was a slow one and there were still hiccups. Before the Oscar awards confirmed his star status again, he was signed for a year only by Capitol Records, with no advances or expenses. His first recording session was with Axel Stordahl and was still in the lush romantic vein of his earlier work. At his second session at the end of April 1953, however, the arranger was Nelson Riddle, who was to become instrumental in the next stage of Sinatra's musical development. Together they recorded their classic version of 'My One and Only Love,' backed by brass and string, and the gradual evolution from crooning to swinging Sinatra was under way.

The European concert tour that followed was less successful, principally because of the ups and downs of the marriage with Ava, which ended in October 1953, although Ava did not finally apply for a divorce until 1957. Frank was devastated by the break-up, which came at Ava's instigation. As she said, 'when he was down and out he was sweet. But now he's got successful again he's become his old arrogant self. We were happy when he was on the skids.' Something of an over-simplification – the chastened Sinatra of the bad years might have been easier to live with, but he certainly wasn't happy living in Ava's shadow, despite the support, both moral and physical, that she gave him. With the resurrection of his career, the famous and not-so-famous courtiers gathered again and Frank seemed to need Ava less. 'Don't cut the corners too close on me, baby,' he warned her, but they were neither of them secure enough to give the other the lee-

*Right:* Sinatra arriving in Los Angeles in November 1953, an emaciated and melancholy figure, after spending several days in a New York hospital suffering from exhaustion and emotional strain. MGM, on Ava's behalf, had announced their impending divorce. Frank joined her at Christmas on location in Europe for *The Barefoot Contessa,* but the reunion was brief.

way each seemed to need, and the conclusion was probably an inevitable one.

Something of the anguish that he felt over the break-up comes through in the songs of the period, giving a new intensity and turbulence to his recordings. 'Don't Worry 'Bout Me,' 'Little Girl Blue,' 'I Get A Kick Out Of You' and 'It's a Blue World' all signal a new mastery of lyrics of loss and loneliness. 'It was Ava who did that, taught him how to sing a torch song,' acccording to Nelson Riddle, 'That's how he learned. She was the greatest love of his life and he lost her.' The swinging, spontaneous ballad style that characterized their music of the 1950s came to be known to Sinatra fans as the Capitol Years. The first big hit was 'Young at Heart,' recorded in December 1953, which shot spectacularly to the top of the singles parade in March 1954, coinciding with the Oscar award ceremony and confirming an equally spectacular comeback.

During the remainder of the 1950s Sinatra recorded some of his most famous numbers and moved successfully into albums, but the years were dominated by acting; he made a total of 17 films. The first of these, *Suddenly*, made in 1954 with United Artists, is also one of the most interesting, and again shows Sinatra's capabilities as an actor when given a part he could get his teeth into. He plays the role of a psychopath assassin who finds his calling in World War II when given a gun and is now being paid $500 000 to kill the president. Reviews were excellent; *Newsweek*, for example, reported that: 'Sinatra superbly refutes the idea that the straight-role potentialities which earned an Academy Award for him in *From Here to Eternity* were one-shot stuff. In *Suddenly* the happy-go-lucky soldier of *Eternity* becomes one of the most repellent killers in American screen history. Sneeringly arrogant in the beginning, brokenly whimpering at the finish, Sinatra will astonish viewers who flatly resent bobbysoxers' idols.' *Cue* was equally impressed: 'He holds the screen and commands it with ease, authority and skill that is, obviously, the result of care, study, work and an intelligent mind.'

As if to prove his versatility, Sinatra went on to make four very different films in the following year. *Young at Heart*, co-starring Doris Day, was a musical remake of *Four Daughters*, with Frank taking the John Garfield role of the brilliant but moody musician. His numbers included the Gershwins' 'Someone to Watch Over Me,' Cole Porter's 'Just One of Those Things' and Harold Arlen and Johnny Mercer's classic 'One For My Baby.' *Not as a Stranger* with Robert Mitchum and Olivia de Havilland was a somewhat improbable hospital soap opera ('the very finest consistency, but still soap,' said *The Saturday Review*), but Frank's role as Mitchum's cheerful and cynical young doctor colleague was much praised.

*Left:* Frank as the tough, dangerous killer in *Suddenly* (1954), a movie that confirmed his star acting status.

*Below:* Sinatra conducts a 56-piece orchestra at a Columbia recording session, with Nelson Riddle on his immediate left. 'He's stimulating to work with,' said Riddle later. 'The man himself somehow draws everything out of you. We know what we're each *doing* with a song . . .'

role of Sky Masterson and Sinatra turning in a nicely-judged casual performance as Nathan Detroit, proprietor of 'the oldest established permanent floating craps game in New York.' The chemistry between the two stars was never easy and their very different working methods – Brando was a method man while Sinatra specialized in the single take – were a constant irritant. 'Don't put me in the game, coach,' he said to director Joseph L Manckiewicz, 'until Mumbles is through rehearsing.' The result earned a favorable review from Louella Parsons in the *Los Angeles Examiner*, healing a rift that dated from the time of his break-up with Nancy.

The commitment that Frank was bringing to his film career at this time is clearest of all in *The Man with the Golden Arm* (1955), where he plays a reformed junkie and would-be drummer who succumbs to another fix and misses his chance at an audition. The high point of the film is the three-day agony of withdrawal the character goes through in his determination to break free of the drug habit. Director Otto Preminger, aware of the physical and emotional demands that the scene made, told Sinatra he could have as many rehearsals and takes as he liked but to his surprise his star shot the whole climax in a single take. The power of his performance was such that it was singled out by critics for praise and he was nominated for another Oscar, but drug addiction was too controversial a subject for many, and the award went to Ernest Borgnine for the title role in *Marty*.

*Above:* With Doris Day in *Young at Heart* Frank's first film release of several in 1955, described by one critic as 'an old-fashioned treat with roses round the door.'

Next came *The Tender Trap*, a thin but endearing comedy with Debbie Reynolds, both less pretentious and, within its more limited scope, much more successful. It moved the heavyweight *New York Times* to commend Sinatra's performance as 'well-nigh a perfect demonstration of the sort of flippant, frantic thing he can do best. It catches the nervous, restless Frankie at the top of his comedy form.' Finally came *Guys and Dolls*, the classic musical based on a story by Damon Runyon, with Marlon Brando in the romantic singing

*Right:* In *The Tender Trap* (1955), popular bachelor Sinatra finally succumbs to the machinations of Debbie Reynolds, a girl with a timetable for matrimony. Here they are pictured with co-stars Celeste Holm and David Wayne.

Nonetheless Sinatra's acting profile was by now so high that United Artists agreed to finance him in independent productions. The first of these was *Johnny Concho*, which he both produced and starred in, but it was not a critical success; the monotonous script and direction undermined Sinatra's perfectly competent playing of a delinquent cowboy. The *Los Angeles Times* reported that: 'The film apparently represents two wish fulfilments of every Hollywood star – to boss his own company and to play a cowboy. Sinatra has, on the whole, done better with the second wish than with the first. Perfectly competently if never brilliantly, he at least causes one to dislike him at the start and pull for him at the finish, which is what one is supposed to do.'

An almost continuous year of filming had to some extent compensated for the emptiness of Sinatra's private life at this time. Jule Styne shared a bachelor apartment with him for much of the time and was less than discreet about the drinking, the depression, the late-night calls to patient ex-wife Nancy and the tanked-up crying jags over Ava. After eight months he was asked to leave and Frank did not speak to him again for five years. Other friends saw a different side of him, however. When Sammy Davis Jr lost his eye in a car accident, Sinatra was his most regular and comforting visitor and later offered his Palm Springs home for convalescence. But the rows with the press continued, and in December 1954 Sinatra set on Mel Tormé's publicist Jim Byron for alerting the Hollywood columnists

to the fact that he was escorting the pregnant Judy Garland to a Tormé concert while her husband was out of town. These were also the years of the Holmby Hills Rat Pack, a group of like-minded anti-establishment friends, admirers of Democrats Roosevelt, Truman and Adlai Stevenson, which tended to congregate round Humphrey Bogart and Lauren Bacall and which included Judy Garland, David Niven and Sammy Cahn as well as Sinatra.

If 1955 was the year of the film for Frank, 1956 was the year of the record. In the previous

*Above:* Sinatra as *The Man with the Golden Arm* (1955) with girlfriend Kim Novak, who helps him through a tortured three-day 'cold turkey' cure for his drug addiction; 'a truly virtuoso performance,' according to *The Saturday Review*, and it won Sinatra an Oscar nomination.

*Left: Guys and Dolls* (1955) paired two very different actors in Sinatra and Brando and the result, though favorably received at the time, was a rather flat, studio-bound movie.

*Above:* Sinatra the recording star; the late 1950s produced a stream of best-selling albums for him.

few years recording had taken second place to filming, but in 1956 he made time for over 20 studio recording sessions. During his bad years the ten-inch LP had been developed, and although Sinatra continued to have many single hits in the 1950s his major success was in the LP charts, selling to adults rather than the more fickle teenage market. This gave him an alternative outlet to the hit parade, now mainly dominated by rock and roll stars, and also allowed him the chance to shine as a compiler as well as performer. Between 1954 and 1961 thirteen 12 inch Sinatra records made with Capitol were top five LPs, nearly all arranged by Nelson Riddle and many of them with a brave eight songs a side. These inevitably cost more, because of the publishers' royalties to be paid on extra songs, but they sold anyway.

The first of these albums, 'Swing Easy' in 1954, had chamber jazz accompaniment; 'In the Wee Small Hours' has been called the first concept album in pop music, with its litany of yearning love songs; 'Songs for Swinging Lovers' in 1956 was perhaps the high point of this development and Riddle's best work. It was a subtle big band album and included numbers like Cole Porter's 'I've Got You Under My Skin,' voted an all-time favorite by fans in 1980, as well as 'You Make Me Feel So Young' and 'You're Getting to be a Habit With Me.' *Metronome* named 'Swinging Lovers' one of the best jazz albums of the year, and a poll of jazz artists named Sinatra their top-choice Musicians' Musician, giving a satisfactory accolade to the new swinging Sinatra. Other LPs that took the late 1950s audience by storm and still continue to sell include 'Come Fly With Me' and 'Only the Lonely' (both 1958 and topping the LP chart); 'Come Dance With Me' (1959); 'Nice 'N' Easy' ( topping the LP charts in 1960) and 'All the Way' (1961), all recorded with Nelson Riddle. Riddle himself said that Sinatra, though never easy to work

*Above:* Sinatra on location, well equipped with Capitol record player and single.

*Left:* Sinatra with fellow Clan members Sammy Davis Jr and Peter Lawford at Davis' wedding to Mae Britt in 1960. The Clan was just one in a series of male support groups that Sinatra collected round him, much to the disapproval of his various wives and girlfriends.

**Right:** Despite his divorce from Nancy, Frank remained in close touch with his ex-wife and their children. Here he is pictured with ten-year-old Christina and eighteen-year-old Nancy junior, whom he delighted in squiring to the occasional Hollywood premiere.

with, brought out his best work: 'He'd pick out all the songs for an album and then call me over to go through them. He'd have very definite ideas about the general treatment, particularly about the pace of the record and which areas should be soft or loud, happy or sad.'

Sinatra was equally complimentary about Riddle: 'Nelson is the greatest arranger in the world. He's like a tranquillizer – calm, slightly aloof. Nothing every ruffles him.' The whole process of planning and producing an LP, the basis for which he had learned from Tommy Dorsey's skill in pacing a show, gave Sinatra particular pleasure and satisfaction. By 1959, however, his relations with his recording studio, Capitol, were less than cordial. His contract was not due for renewal until 1962

and when Sinatra asked to be released Capitol at first refused, although in the end a deal was struck, with Sinatra agreeing to do four more albums in exchange for his independence. One of his companies already had copyright in Sinatra's master tapes, and it seems likely that recording independence had been on the cards for some time.

This musical emphasis reappears in some of the films Sinatra made in 1956, notably *High Society*, a musical remake of the classic *Philadelphia Story*, starring Sinatra, Grace Kelly and Bing Crosby in the roles previously taken by James Stewart, Katharine Hepburn and Cary Grant. The new version may not have quite the style of the original, but Cole Porter's songs and the presence of Louis Armstrong

playing himself, of course, make it a thoroughly enjoyable romp – and the cast clearly had a wonderful time making it. The duet 'What a Swell Party' with Bing Crosby scores a new high in musical comedy routines, and the nicknames 'Nembutal' and 'Dexedrine' for Crosby and Sinatra respectively give some indication of the animated atmosphere on set.

By contrast *The Pride and the Passion*, based on C S Forester's novel *The Gun* and set in Spain during the Peninsular War against Napoleon, was hard work in an uncongenial environment. Co-starring Sophia Loren and Cary Grant, the film was shot in 16 gruelling weeks on location in Spain and while most of the crew and cast, including Grant and Loren, made do with accommodation on location, Sinatra insisted on staying in Madrid and driving sometimes hundreds of miles for each day's shoot. Not that he showed any lack of commitment once on set – producer Stanley Kramer said 'I had him trudging up and down mountains, wading in rivers, crawling in mud from one end of Spain to the other, and he never complained once.' It was the usual problem of hanging around while other actors rehearsed and crowd scenes were set up. Sophia Loren found him easy to get on with: 'Here he is kindly, friendly. He has even helped me with my English, has taught me how people really speak in Hollywood. He is a regular gasser. I dig him.' But the reputation that Sinatra earned for being difficult on set may

**Right:** Bing Crosby, Grace Kelly and Sinatra in *High Society*. Sinatra, as brash and idealistic young photographer Mike Connor, first despises and then falls for Kelly's society belle Tracy Lord.

**Below:** Sinatra uncomfortably miscast as a Spanish peasant turned guerrilla leader in *The Pride and the Passion* (1957), killing time on location in Spain with co-star Sophia Loren.

well have prevented more challenging and exciting offers from coming his way in the future.

His next two film roles were closer to home, both in terms of the character Sinatra played and in the sense that they were productions part-owned by a Sinatra company. *The Joker is Wild* is a version of Sinatra's own downfall and recovery and was critically well received; the *Los Angeles Times* commented that 'He has the outer mannerisms down pat and catches the bitter inner restlessness almost too well.' *Pal Joey*, co-starring Rita Hayworth and Kim Novak, was originally a Rodgers and Hart stage musical and included 'The Lady is a Tramp' among its numbers. His latest venture into television, however, a major series for which ABC paid him $3 million, again ploughed. The first 13 musical half-hours were shot in less than 20 days and it showed. The *New Yorker* described it as 'under-organized and a little desperate;' the laid-back attitude that worked for Sinatra on film could not hold a whole television series together.

The movies of the late 1950s also got a mixed reception. *Kings Go Forth*, a rather heavy-going war melodrama co-starring Tony Curtis and Natalie Wood, was praised by the *Los Angeles Examiner*: 'The Thin Singer has never had a more difficult role and he has never more completely mastered a characterization. Might as well admit it, he's a great actor.' But *Films and Filming* thought differently: '*Kings Go Forth*, glib, happy ending and all, really is the limit. It is time someone debunked this kind of specious, hysterical

*Left:* Director Stanley Kramer gives Sinatra some last-minute instructions before shooting a night scene in the Spanish town of Valdemoro for *The Pride and the Passion.*

*Below:* Spanish insurrectionists Sinatra and Loren and British naval officer Cary Grant join forces against the Napoleonic troops occupying the town of Avila. They have dragged their monster gun into position outside the walls and prepare to attack at dawn.

liberalism.' *Some Came Running*, released the following year, was also coolly received. Sinatra played the ex-soldier returning home to more trouble, with Dean Martin and old friend Shirley MacLaine as the tart with the heart of gold whom he finally marries, only to see her killed by a jealous ex-boyfriend. *Time* said dismissively: 'As bromide follows bromide, the spectator slowly comes to a drugged realization that the script is not making fun of anybody's beliefs, but simply stating its own. After that there is nothing to hang around for except occasional flickers of brilliant overacting by Shirley MacLaine, the chance to watch Frank Sinatra play Frank Sinatra, and the spectacle of director Vincente Minnelli's talents dissolving in the general mess . . . '

*Some Came Running* also marked a new low in Sinatra's relations with the press. After Bogart's death he was seen increasingly in the company of Bogart's widow Lauren Bacall, which led to constant speculation in the showbiz press about the likelihood of a marriage. Bacall said later of the relationship: 'It worked out marvellously for a while until the press went absolutely mad and drove both of us mad.' On location in Indiana to make *Some Came Running*, the cast as a whole and Sinatra in particular came in for much criticism for antagonizing a small conservative isolated community; the press gladly reported Sinatra's and Martin's preference for gambling over the border in Kentucky rather than attending a

**Above:** Sinatra as the promising young singer Joe Lewis who survives mobster attack to make it as a stand-up comic, with co-star Mitzi Gaynor in *The Joker is Wild* (1957).

**Right:** With Shirley MacLaine in *Some Came Running* (1958).

**Opposite:** On the set of *Pal Joey* (1957). Sinatra was sensitive about his receding hairline and was rarely seen without a hat.

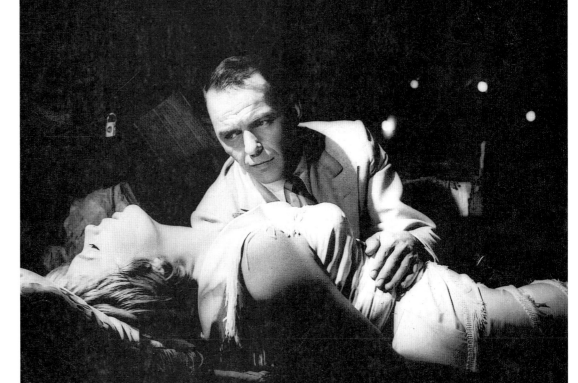

**Right:** Sinatra with Kim Novak in *Pal Joey*. 'One of the few musical comedies on record with a little heel as a hero,' as *Look* magazine put it.

**Left and below:** *High Society* teamed Crosby and Sinatra as two men after the same girl – the rich and glamorous Tracy Lord (Grace Kelly).

local dance – a taste for which modern readers might not be so ready to condemn them. Sinatra's next film, *A Hole in the Head* with Edward G Robinson, came under similar fire; the local press homed in on stories about Sinatra's preference for parties over work and his rows with his co-star, although studio head Joe Hyams found no evidence for these when he visited the set. Neither of his 1959 films, *Never So Few* and *Can-Can*, were great hits, despite the latter's Cole Porter songs, choreography by Hermes Pan and the urbane presence of Maurice Chevalier as the righteous lawyer who falls for can-can dancer Shirley MacLaine.

Part of the problem as far as the press was concerned was Sinatra's visibly successful business acumen. Soon after winning his Oscar for *From Here to Eternity*, Frank was finally approved for a Nevada state gambling license. It was over 14 months before the State Tax Commission gave its blessing, partly out of concern about possible underworld associations. At that time there were only half a

dozen hotels on the Las Vegas strip but it was the only place in the USA that offered legalized casino gambling; when Frank bought a two percent interest in one of those hotels he knew he could not lose. As he said at the time, 'When I am finished as an entertainer I want to have an investment that will ensure the education of my children and a sufficient income for me. I think this Sands investment will keep me very comfortably.' In fact his gambling license was eventually to make him a multimillionaire, quite apart from the phenomenal fees he could command as a performer. In the course of the 1950s he created a substantial financial empire, including his film production company Essex Films, four music publishing companies, radio station partnerships with Danny Kaye, and plenty of real estate.

If that was not enough to make him fair press game, his continuing romances certainly were. The affair with Bacall was closely followed by one with London society beauty Lady Adele Beatty, a more discreet liaison with Marilyn Monroe, and the much-publicized engagement to Juliet Prowse, who first met Sinatra when she also worked on *Can-Can*. This relationship survived a succession of other dates and affairs over a period of two years, until finally at the end of 1961 Sinatra proposed – only to call the whole thing off six weeks later because his fiancée was unwilling to give up her career.

# Chapter 5
# KING OF SWING
## *1961-*

THE last thirty years have seen Sinatra both peak and plummet in almost every aspect of his career. There have been excellent films and appallingly self-indulgent ones; public accolades and public rows; romances and bust-ups. But the hard times of the late 1940s have never been repeated and Sinatra the multi-millionaire has comfortably survived the occasional press panning. Above all his records continue to sell in staggering numbers and since 1961, when he finally shook free of Capitol and set up his own independent recording company, Reprise Records, a substantial proportion of the profits have been ploughed back.

When he founded Reprise, Sinatra announced that the public would be hearing 'a new, happier, emancipated Sinatra, untrammeled, unfettered, unconfined.' In fact the early days were distinctly shaky, especially when Capitol took the fledgling company to court, alleging that its second Sinatra album, 'Swing Along With Me,' closely resembled their 'Come Swing With Me.' The complaint was upheld and the title of the Reprise album changed. It was Sinatra's turn to sue in the following year, 1962, when a discounting war led to allegations of restraint of trade. Again he lost, but the net result of the well-publicized competition was to boost Capitol's record sales to the point where Sinatra's royalties offset Reprise's losses, and the four new albums he issued with Reprise in 1962 all became instant bestsellers, ensuring the recording company's survival.

The high recording standards that Sinatra demanded in these early recordings helped to enhance Reprise's reputation. In the first year

he is supposed to have rejected more master tapes than in any equivalent period throughout his career. Nelson Riddle was still under contract to Capitol, so Sinatra experimented with a number of other arranger/conductors, including Billy May, Sy Oliver, Don Costa and Neal Hefti, who had worked with Count

*Opposite:* Sinatra in relaxed mood in this publicity shot from 1961.

*Left:* Sinatra holds the special Oscar he received in 1971, the Jean Hersholt humanitarian award for charitable activities.

Basie. Riddle's return to the fold in 1963 was celebrated with 'The Concert Sinatra' and, one of the most successful Riddle albums of all, 'Sinatra's Sinatra.' A more novel development was the collaboration with Count Basie and his orchestra. Even in his early recording, such as 'The Things We Did Last Summer,' Frank's relaxed phrasing and rhythmic sensitivity had won him the admiration of jazz fans, and the 'Sinatra-Basie' album saw Sinatra the jazz singer at his peak.

Reprise rapidly collected a satisfactory stable of talented recording stars, including Bing Crosby, Dean Martin and Sammy Davis Jr, attracted by high standards, ownership of their own master-tapes, and the freedom to organize their own recording sessions. By mid 1963 the company was so healthy that Jack Warner made Sinatra an irresistible $10 million offer under which Reprise merged with Warner's recording company, leaving Sinatra with one third ownership, recording freedom and a film deal. Sinatra had always found it easy to spend money but some of the wildest extravagances – the hundred-dollar tips to hatcheck girls, the round-the-world flights for

friends, the suitcases full of cash – date from the 1960s. But then so do the charity concerts and tours. Between 1960 and 1962 the Sinatra empire spent over a quarter of a million dollars on two series of charity concerts in Mexico and a two-month charity tour of Europe and Japan which raised over a million dollars profit for the charities concerned.

The 1960s were also the Clan Years. After Bogart's death the Holmby Hills Rat Pack lost its zest, and the group that gradually grew up round Sinatra was rather different in character. Like similar groups earlier in Sinatra's career, the so-called Clan was primarily an association of business partners – longtime friend and colleague Hank Sanicola, film star Peter Lawford, songwriters Sammy Cahn and Jimmy van Heusen, and performers Dean Martin, Sammy Davis Jr and Joey Bishop. Clan traditions developed out of the night club routines performed by the central trio of Sinatra, Martin and Davis and gave rise in the early 1960s to a series of lightweight, self-indulgent and variably entertaining Clan movies. The first of these was *Oceans Eleven*, made in Las Vegas in 1960. The local press

*Below:* The Crooner and the Swooner in front of the television cameras for Frank's ABC show. In 1962 he joined a 'Hope/Crosby 'Road' movie, *The Road to Hong Kong*, as guest artist.

*Left:* Another honored guest on the *Frank Sinatra Show* was Mrs Eleanor Roosevelt, widow of the Democrat President, here shown chatting with her host during rehearsal. The date was November 2, 1960, days before the presidential election; Frank was an ardent Kennedy supporter.

were astounded by the hectic pace at which the group lived. They filmed every morning, and Sinatra also shot a cameo role in *Pepe* in the afternoon and rehearsed for a forthcoming television show in the early evening; then they all moved on stage for two late-night shows at the Sands Hotel. Sammy Davis Jr recalls in his memoirs that for eight weeks the Sands was the center of the American entertainment business; so exhausting was the schedule that he spent a week in hospital afterward. He also makes clear the extent to which Sinatra was the moving force behind the group – it was his idea to make an annual film, and the result was *Sergeants Three* (1962), *Four for Texas* (1963) and *Robin and the Seven Hoods* (1964).

These were also the Kennedy years and Sinatra, always a committed Democrat, became deeply involved in the fight to get Kennedy into the White House. In 1954 Peter Lawford had married Patricia Kennedy and from the following year Sinatra was involved in a series of meetings to build support for the Kennedy nomination throughout California.

*Left:* Sinatra with Jacqueline Kennedy; his irresistible attraction to the Democrats was his potential as a fundraiser. Initial doubts about his suitability as a campaign weapon were temporarily allayed by his civil rights reputation, but the Kennedy dream did not last long for Sinatra.

57

**Right:** Frank, with Sammy Davis Jr and Dean Martin horse around between takes of *Sergeants Three* (1962), second of the Clan movies and very loosely based on a Rudyard Kipling story; 'the ghost of Rudyard Kipling must be whirling like a dervish in its grave,' said one unimpressed critic.

**Below:** The singing Sinatra on stage at his Madison Square Garden concert in 1971.

Sinatra was immensely impressed by the young, brilliant, charismatic Senator, and Kennedy in turn enjoyed the Hollywood high life that Frank laid on for him. But almost from the beginning the association was a troubled one for Sinatra. In March 1960 the *New York Times* broke the news that Sinatra was planning to hire as a screenwriter the novelist Albert Maltz, who had already written the award-winning anti-racism short *The House I Live In*. Since then, however, Maltz had been blacklisted as one of the 'Hollywood Ten,' and fined and imprisoned for refusing to testify to the House Un-American Activities Committee during the anti-Communist witch-hunt years. The press furore was extraordinary. 'Dump Maltz and get yourself a true American,' thundered the *Los Angeles Examiner*; 'If Sinatra loves his country he won't do this,' lamented the *Los Angeles Times*. Torn between his commitment to exposing the hypocrisy of the Hollywood blacklist and his reluctance to damage the Kennedy election campaign, Sinatra finally gave way and abandoned the project; a sadly ironic retreat.

At the Democratic Convention, held in Los Angeles in July 1960, Sinatra and the Clan opened the ceremonies singing 'The Star-Spangled Banner,' and after the election Frank

*Above:* Sinatra at the high point of his relationship with the Kennedys escorts the glamorous Jackie up to her box for the pre-inauguration gala he staged in January 1961 to help pay off the Kennedy campaign debt.

*Left:* Sinatra, Davis and Martin in 1988, rehearsing for a 29-city tour.

organized an epic inauguration gala in Washington which outstripped all others in the breadth of talent present, a testimony to his showbiz stature. It is possible that he was hoping for some political recognition – Hollywood gossip, less than seriously, had it that he would be appointed Ambassador to Italy, but the inauguration proved the high point of his relations with the Kennedys. Even before the election the Republican press were full of smear stories connecting Sinatra and the Clan with the underworld. With Bobby Kennedy's decision as Attorney General to declare war on the Mafia, Frank's days of acceptability to the White House were numbered. Within weeks of the inauguration Bobby was advising his brother that Frank had too many friends and contacts in the Mafia world to be safe company. The heliport that Frank had built in his Palm springs compound to welcome a vacationing President was never used for its intended purpose and by 1962 the Kennedy honeymoon was over, leaving Sinatra bitter and disappointed and ripe to turn Republican.

More trouble came in 1963, with a confrontation with the Nevada State Gaming Board. Three years earlier the Board had circulated a list of eleven 'known gangsters' who were to be banned from any Nevada gambling enterprise. One of those listed was Sinatra's longtime friend Sam Giancana, so when he stayed at Sinatra's Cal-Neva gambling lodge the Board threatened to withdraw Sinatra's gaming license. The Board's blacklist was well known to be selective – it did not include any

*Above and right:* The kidnapping of Frank Jr in 1963 united the Sinatra family in their anxiety for his safety. Frank Jr, his mother and his grandparents Dolly and Marty (*below*) are shown at press conferences after Frank's release unharmed.

*Opposite:* The critical moment in *The Manchurian Candidate* (1962) when Sinatra works out that the key to controling his brainwashed colleague Laurence Harvey is the Queen of Diamonds.

**Right:** Sinatra with Tony Bill as the riotous Baker brothers in *Come Blow Your Horn* (1963)

**Opposite:** In cheerful mood on the set of *Von Ryan's Express* (1965), in which Sinatra's role as steely-eyed, curt and unpopular Colonel Ryan was much praised.

**Below:** A mood shot of Sinatra on a rocky seashore with the script of *None But the Brave*, a not wholly successful anti-war melodrama.

of the mobsters who actually had a stake in Nevada's casinos – and Frank got a lot of support. As one commentator said: 'For Nevada – by God, Nevada! – to go high and mighty . . . is the absolute Chinese end.' Sinatra was given two weeks to answer the charges of associating with a Mafia boss and, to the surprise of many, he again withdrew, selling his holdings in the Cal-Neva and Sands casinos.

A bad year ended with the assassination of President Kennedy and the kidnapping three weeks later of Frank Jr, who had just launched out on a professional singing career. This proved a fairly amateur undertaking; Frank senior paid the required ransom and one of the kidnappers gave himself up shortly after. Suggestions at the trial that the kidnapping had been a publicity stunt were given no credence by the jury, and Sinatra was awarded substantial damages in a British court when similar allegations were made on British television.

As well as the Clan movies the 1960s saw some serious Sinatra films, though again of variable quality. *The Manchurian Candidate* was one of the best of these, a wildly plotted but well handled spy thriller in which ex-Korean prisoner-of-war Sinatra gradually realizes that he and fellow prisoner Raymond

Shaw (chillingly played by British actor Laurence Harvey) have been brainwashed, and that Harvey has been programmed for a suicide mission. *The New Yorker* hailed it with 'Many loud hurrahs . . . a thriller guaranteed to raise all but the limpest hair . . . The acting is all of a high order, and Sinatra, in his usual uncanny fashion, is simply terrific.' Even the highly critical Pauline Kael, writing in the mid 1970s, allowed that 'It may be the most sophisticated political satire ever to come out of Hollywood.'

*Come Blow Your Horn*, a somewhat solid transcription to film of an early Neil Simon Broadway success, was also well received the following year, but the freedom that owning his own production companies gave Sinatra did not produce the right material. *None But the Brave*, yet another war movie made in 1965, is interesting for its admirable anti-war message and the fact that Sinatra directed as well as starred, but it got mixed reviews – *Time* commented that 'The idea holds some promise, except that director Sinatra and his scriptwriters goof away tension at every turn.' Perhaps Sinatra was discouraged by the movie's reception, or maybe directing was a one-off experiment in his fiftieth year; either way it was his one foray. His next film was the much more successful *Von Ryan's Express*, a fast-moving thriller set in an Italian prisoner-of-war camp and co-starring Trevor Howard. An ill-assorted Anglo-American group of prisoners, including Colonel Ryan (Sinatra), nicknamed 'von' for his apparently Nazi sympathies, seize a train and make a dash for the Swiss border; the train chase and the nail-biting finale are classics of the genre.

In the mid-1960s Sinatra's private life again came to the forefront of press attention with his relationship with Mia Farrow. In the ten years since he had broken off his engagment to Juliet Prowse, only Jill St John among an endless stream of attractive women had shown any staying power, and Sinatra seemed destined for permanent bachelordom. Mia, whom he met on the Twentieth Century Fox lot while shooting *Von Ryan's Express*, was quite a change. Thirty years younger than Frank, she was already a star in her own right with her part in the television serial *Peyton Place*; one of the new generation of independent, sophisticated young women, she was into meditation and healthy eating. They seemed an unlikely pair and the press were fascinated. When they went on holiday together in summer 1965, *Time* suggested that it was 'the most closely observed cruise since Cleopatra floated down the Nile to meet Mark Antony.'

In July 1966 they married, and almost at once ran into problems with clashing work schedules. Sinatra simply could not accept that his wife's work commitments might need to take precedence over his requirements. When Mia's role in *Rosemary's Baby* ran over schedule, overlapping with Frank's film *The Detective* in which she also had a part, he told her to walk off her picture. When she refused he gave her part to Jacqueline Bisset and

*Right:* Sinatra in his favorite western dress, with Mia Farrow at a fundraising party in spring 1965. She still has the long hair which characterized her role of Alison Mackenzie in *Peyton Place*. In December, within a week of Sinatra's fiftieth birthday which he spent first with Nancy and the children and then in private with Mia, she had her hair shorn to its more familiar *garçon* look. Her friend and mentor Salvador Dali called the gesture 'mythical suicide'.

**Left:** Frank and Mia on their wedding day in July 1966. The relationship ran into storms almost at once; Frank still expected an old-fashioned, low-key, subordinate wife, whereas Mia was a self-respecting, self-financing star. Frank in love, even at fifty, was acknowledged to be an overwhelming charmer but marriage proved a different story. Four weeks after the wedding Frank had a nightclub engagement at the Sands Hotel, Las Vegas. 'Maybe you wondered why I finally got married,' he said to his audience. 'Well, I finally found a broad I can cheat on.' The remark may have been meant as a joke but it reduced Mia to tears.

announced the end of the marriage. Ironically *The Detective* is the best of Sinatra's later films. He plays a tough New York cop who gradually uncovers a complex web of corruption that has caused him to send an innocent man to the chair. Determinedly violent and sleazy, the film nonetheless has something interesting to say about police methods; when third degree fails, Sinatra elicits a (false, as it turns out) confession by persuasion. Two other late

**Right:** Sinatra in action again in his role as a detective with the New York police department following a series of film successes which began with *The Detective*. This one was a made-for-television special called *Contract on Cherry Street*. 'The bird-brained plot' noted the *New York Times* 'proves fatal to all concerned.'

**Opposite:** Sinatra in January 1974, a few months after his 'retirement from retirement' was heralded by the release of a new album, 'Ol' Blue Eyes is Back' and a television show of the same name. He followed this up with a successful return to the cabaret circuit at Caesar's Palace in Las Vegas, playing eight one-hour shows.

thrillers, *Tony Rome* and its sequel *Lady in Cement*, follow similar lines, this time with Sinatra as a private eye investigating an old-fashioned murder mystery plus a fashionable helping of sex and violence.

The late 1960s also saw some classic recordings. 1965, his fiftieth year, was a good one, with a Grammy award for the introspective album 'September of My Years' and a record-breaking appearance with Count Basie at the Newport Jazz Festival. Sinatra also had his first Top Ten hit since the 1950s with 'It Was a Very Good Year,' while in 1966 'Strangers in the Night' soared straight to the top of the charts, to be followed by 'That's Life' and 'Something Stupid,' an amazing achievement in an intensely competitive singles market that seemed to have left swing way behind. Three

original albums with Don Costa followed in 1968 and 1969, returning to the introspective mood of 'September of My Years.' Two of these, 'Cycles' and 'My Way,' made gold albums.

The announcement of his retirement in 1971 came as a shock to those fans who had assumed that he would keep singing till he dropped, and certainly did not remove his name from the limelight. A final and spectacular mobster showdown, this time with the House Select Committee on Crime in 1972, ended with a triumph for Sinatra. In 1973 he announced his retirement from retirement, and thereafter emerged from seclusion from time to time to do a series of shows. And nothing stopped him from recording. Or from fighting – he showed no sign of mellowing with

**Left:** Sinatra's fourth marriage, to Barbara Marx, was celebrated in May 1976 at the Palm Springs home of Walter Annenberg, former US Ambassador to the Court of St James. The groom's present to the bride was a Rolls-Royce, the bride's to the groom a Jaguar XJS.

age, breaking his front teeth in 1967, aged 52, in a fight with the casino manager of his own hotel, the Sands, and bitterly offending the Australian press on a 1974 comeback tour, earning the accolade 'Sour Apple of the Year' from the Lady Journalists of Hollywood. But if he continued as combative as ever, his private life was improved by the presence of Barbara Marx, who left husband Zeppo of Marx Brothers fame to move into Frank's luxurious Palm Springs retreat. She finally married him in 1976, six years later, just in time to help him through the trauma when the private jet bringing his mother, the irrepressible Dolly, to Las Vegas disappeared shortly after take-off. As a direct result of his mother's death, Sinatra agreed to a screen comeback making his first-ever television movie, *Contract on Cherry Street*, based on Dolly's favorite novel and in which he plays an anti-Mafia cop.

And still the recordings flowed, though now at longer intervals. 'Trilogy: Past, Present,

Future' was a top-20 three-album set in 1980; in the same year his single 'Theme From New York New York' made it into the top 40; while in 1985 'LA is My Lady' made Billboard's 'adult contemporary' list. His 75th birthday tour in 1990 was not only, and inevitably, a sell-out, but also a critical triumph. The easy singing style, the one-to-one banter, the mastery of the live performance, still retained their power to charm and inspire audiences worldwide. Like him or loathe him, and Sinatra continues to provoke extreme reactions, there is no doubting the fact that he has created his own unique niche on the popular musical scene of the twentieth century. As the London *Evening Standard* wrote when he played the Albert Hall in 1977: 'Behind him he leaves three decades of beautifully sung songs, three decades of nostalgia and bucketfuls of maidenly tears. While Sinatra records are still being played around the world we'll all be romantics from time to time.'

**Opposite:** Frank in performance with daughter Nancy. Always her father's most devoted fan, Nancy had a chart-topping hit of her own in 1965 with 'These Boots Were Made for Walking.' In 1967 father and daughter together made it to number one in both England and the US with 'Something Stupid.'

**Left:** Sinatra tanned and relaxed in the late 1970s, after his marriage to Barbara Marx.

**Right:** After Kennedy's assassination Sinatra lost enthusiasm for the Democrat cause, and this 1980 picture shows him firmly entrenched in the Reagan era. There are even wild rumors of an affair with the First Lady.

**Below:** In 1988 Liza Minnelli, daughter of Judy Garland, stepped in for an ill Dean Martin during a Sinatra/Davis tour.

To celebrate Frank Sinatra's eightieth birthday in 1995, Reprise Records released a massive 20-CD retrospective collection of everything he had recorded for the label. Known as *'The Complete Reprise Studio Recordings'*, it was a limited edition, 454-song set sequenced for the most part in chronological order from 1960 to 1988 — with a 96-page hardcover book — that sold for $700. Seventy of the songs were previously unavailable on CD, and 18 had never been released, including a disco version of 'All Or Nothing At All.'

Meanwhile, Columbia released its own retrospective package, entitled *'Frank Sinatra: The Best Of The Columbia Years 1943-1952.'* It was an impressive 97-song, four-CD set with a 70-page, full color inserted book. In Sinatra's own introduction to the accompany-

ing book, he wrote that 'For me, it began at Columbia.'

Capitol, his other label, released *'Sinatra Eightieth: All The Best,'* a 40-song, two-CD set compiled from recordings he made from 1953 to 1962, including 'Come Fly With Me,' 'The Lady Is A Tramp' and 'I've Got You Under My Skin.' The highlight from this package was, of course, an electronic duet between the Chairman of the Board and Nat King Cole on 'The Christmas Song.'

Meanwhile a live album was also released. Entitled *'Sinatra Eightieth: Live In Concert,'* it was a 15-song collection of his newer songs that was recorded during concerts that he gave in the eighties. Among the songs were 'You Are The Sunshine Of My Life' and a duet with Luciano Pavarotti on 'My Way.'

In addition to 'The Complete Reprise Studio Recordings,' Reprise also released a a single CD entitled 'Everything Happens to Me,' which was a collection of his own favorite songs which he selected himself. According to a Reprise spokesman, the retrospectives were released because, even in retirement, Sinatra was a mainstay of the music business. Indeed, he would sell one million albums during 1996 alone, according to SoundScan, a company that measures music sales.

In 1995, the Chairman of the Board had announced that he was taking a break from performing to spend more time with his wife, family and friends. However, when it came time for his eightieth birthday celebration, it would be done his way and it would be a birthday bash to remember.

On October 12, 1995, as Frank Sinatra was two months short of celebrating his eightieth birthday, the word went out that tickets were to be put on sale for a star-studded birthday extravaganza to be held on November 19. It would be the centerpiece of an ABC Tele-vision Network special in prime time that was to be known as 'Sinatra: 80 Years My Way.'

Interest in the event was keen. Suzanne Gordon and Ellen Gonzalez at ABC Media Relations in Los Angeles handled a flood of media inquiries as did Susan Reynolds on Mr. Sinatra's staff. The network was excited about the upcoming event, remarking in a press bulletin that it was 'proud to be part of Ol' Blue Eyes' eightieth birthday.'

Tickets near the stage were available from Events Unlimited, Inc. and ranged in price from $250 to $1,000, while more eco-nomical seats were available for $50 and $100. It was a sell-out. The network and the fans were clearly excited about the all-star cel-ebration of Frank Sinatra's birthday and plans were put in place for the televised celebration to be accompanied by a retrospective of the Chairman's spectacular career.

The two-hour, prime time special, scheduled to be aired the week of Frank Sina-tra's actual eightieth birthday on December 12, was to be one of the most important single

events to be aired on the ABC Television Network during 1995. The network knew it, the fans knew it and Frank Sinatra knew it. Indeed, it was the most important Frank Sinatra event of the decade and everyone who was anyone would be there.

Produced by George Schlatter Productions, 'Sinatra: 80 Years My Way' would benefit the Barbara Sinatra Children's Center at the Eisenhower Medical Center in Rancho Mirage, California. The center had been founded by Frank Sinatra and his wife Bar-

bara in 1986 as a place at which to treat and counsel abused children.

'Sinatra: 80 Years My Way' would also benefit the AIDS Project Los Angeles, a charity that was at the time offering more than 30 programs including food, counseling, shelter and dental services to more than 5,200 clients with HIV and AIDS.

On Sunday, November 19, after a month of behind-the-scenes preparation, the friends of the Chairman of the Board, along with fellow recording artists, film, television, and

Left: Frank Sinatra on stage at a sold-out performance in New York's Carnegie Hall on December 14, 1986, the eve of his seventy-first birthday, The photo is courtesy of UPI.

sports celebrities, and various international leaders arrived at the legendary Shrine Auditorium in Los Angeles.

Many of the world's most popular artists participated in 'Sinatra: 80 Years My Way.' Among those who joined Frank Sinatra on stage that night were Bruce Springsteen, Bob Dylan, Little Richard, Hootie And The Blofish, Salt-n-Pepa, Tony Bennett, Patti LaBelle and Natalie Cole.

At 7:15 pm, taping of Ol' Blue Eyes' eightieth birthday show began, reaching its climax when he sang 'My Way' to the packed house. The standing ovation said that his way was also their way and everyone was glad to be on hand for this milestone event.

The Chairman of the Board's exceptional career was profiled through performances and film clips that paid tribute to his Oscar and Emmy award-winning performances, his countless Grammy awards, and his generous philanthropic activities.

As often occurs on birthdays, especially milestone birthdays such as Frank Sinatra's

eightieth birthday, thoughts turn to the stars — not the stars that gathered at Shrine Auditorium on November 19, 1995, but the stars that form the signs of the zodiac. The Philadelphia Daily News got into the act of interpreting the horoscope of the Chairman of the Board, noting that Frank Sinatra had 'left women swooning for more than four generations. With his Sun and Mercury in fiery Sagittarius and Mars in show-stopping Leo, he easily communicates his passion for life through the intensity of his voice and his deep baby blue eyes. With his emotional Moon in sensitive Pisces, setting boundaries is most likely not Sinatra's strong suit, especially when it comes to those closest to him.'

One of the biggest of the actual parties thrown for Frank Sinatra's eightieth birthday was the one held on December 14 at New York's Waldorf Astoria Hotel. It was organized by Capitol Records to mark his long association with that label during his 60-year career. Among the select list of guests were his friends Tony Bennett, Faye Dunaway, Jessye Norman, Diana Ross and Robert Wagner.

The airing of 'Sinatra: 80 Years My Way' and the celebration of his actual birthday on December 15, 1995, were a time of joy and excitement, which left Frank Sinatra, his family and circle of friends in a joyous and upbeat mood as Christmas approached. However, the mood was very soon to change.

On the day after Christmas, that same circle of friends was stunned to learn of the death, on December 26, 1995, of Dean Martin. It was as though Frank Sinatra had lost his brother. Their famous 'Rat Pack' days of Las Vegas in the early sixties were long over, but not even Dean Martin's death could shatter the friendship of decades.

There were tears in the famous blue eyes when, speaking shortly after Dean Martin's funeral, Frank Sinatra told the media that 'Too many times I've been asked to say something about friends who are gone — this is one of the hardest. Dean was my brother — not through blood, but through choice.'

'He has been like the air I breathe — always there, always close by,' the Chairman of the Board said with obvious sadness.

Frank Sinatra's comments on the

passing of the great Dean Martin were echoed by those of longtime friend Alan King. 'Dean and I were friends 52 years. He was crazy. He was so funny, so spirited. He was such great fun to be with when he was young,' King said. 'He was never the same after his son Dino died in a 1987 plane crash . . . He went downhill, you know, after his son went out. Everyone who knows him agrees with that. That took whatever spirit he had out of him.'

In 1996, the Chairman of the Board kept his public appearances to a minimum. 'Sinatra: 80 Years My Way' had been enough for the time being. In February 1996, however, he did make an appearance at the eighth annual Frank Sinatra Celebrity Golf Tournament, held at Palm Desert, California. How could he not? His friends were getting together and it was his tournament.

Begun in 1988, the Frank Sinatra Celebrity Golf Tournament was a benefit meet that brought together many Sinatra friends, fellow recording artists, film, television and sports celebrities, as well as professional golfers whose names were known on the PGA tour. Former President Gerald Ford, actors Clint Eastwood, Robert Wagner and James Woods, and astronauts Alan Shepard and Buzz Aldrin are among celebrities who have played in the annual tournament.

The February 1996 event raised $700,000 to benefit the Barbara Sinatra Children's Center at the Eisenhower Medical Center, one of the Sinatras' favorite charities.

The Barbara Sinatra Children's Center has maintained its fight to provide quality treatment and counseling for abused children at a time when government funding for counseling programs is in peril. The center counsels more than 625 children and families at the Center each year, regardless of their ability to pay. During the fiscal year 1996 alone, the Center provided 15,120 client hours of child sexual abuse treatment, 682 client hours of care for child physically abuse treatment, 381 client hours for pregnant and parent teen counseling, and 2,102 client hours for home-based family intervention.

Treatment at the Barbara Sinatra Children's Center involves everyone affected by the trauma. Both child victims and family members, as well as offenders and adults molested as children, receive treatment that incorporates self-help programs with professional therapy. The Center also serves as a regional diagnostic center to determine and document alleged sexual abuse cases for court purposes. During 1996, the Center would provide 39 evidentiary medical examinations of alleged victims of child sexual abuse.

On the evening of February 10, 1996, Ol' Blue Eyes and his wife Barbara joined their friend, comedian Bob Hope, on stage at a special tribute held as part of the Frank Sinatra Celebrity Golf Tournament. Dubbed 'Frank Sinatra: An American Treasure — Thanks From His Friends and Neighbors,' the event was reminiscent of ABC Television's 1995 'Sinatra: 80 Years My Way,' but the Palm Desert program was more intimate — just 'friends and neighbors' — hundreds of friends and neighbors.

Meanwhile, down the road on Vine Street in Hollywood, a mural sponsored by the Sinatra Society of America was painted on a building across the street from the Capitol Records tower. Created by artist George Sportelli it immortalized Frank Sinatra's face within view of the headquarters of the recording company that immortalized his voice. The 21-foot black-and-white image featured a young Sinatra wearing a felt hat. Around the portrait was a black, gold and white border with lettering that read, 'Sinatra: The voice of the decades.'

While Frank Sinatra's eightieth birthday had been the occasion of a monumental party, his eighty-first was a good deal more low key. This is not to say, however, that it went unnoticed. Quite the contrary, there were tributes galore. One of the most visible accolades received by Ol' Blue Eyes was in New York City, where the top of the Empire State Building was illuminated in blue in his honor.

Across the Hudson River, in his New Jersey hometown, the Hoboken Historical Museum unveiled a sidewalk plaque in front of what remains of his birthplace on Monroe Street. The people of Hoboken had decided to install the plaque because visitors to the site were disappointed that there was no marker, said Robert Forster, president of the Hoboken Historical Museum. The home where Sinatra was born in 1915 had burned down years before, leaving only a brick wall, a wooden door and a brick-and-stucco arch.

Meanwhile, Frank's daughter Nancy, appearing on ABC Television's 'Turning Point' program, was asked what he wanted for his eighty-first birthday. 'You'll never guess,' she replied, 'Another birthday. Isn't that sweet?' He would have his wish.

Just as fans thought that they had seen it all, an exciting new archival discovery was made. In January 1997, the only known film footage of a television performance by Frank Sinatra, Dean Martin and Sammy Davis, Jr. together was discovered in a secretary's closet and donated to the Museum of Television & Radio.

The film — of a 1965 benefit performance for a St. Louis halfway house — was telecast via closed circuit to a handful of movie theaters. In their show, the trio performed such tunes as 'Fly Me to the Moon' and 'Luck Be a Lady.' Johnny Carson filled in for fellow Rat-Packer Joey Bishop.

By this time, however, dark clouds had started to gather. It was toward the end of 1996 that health problems began to stalk the Chairman of the Board. In November, Sinatra was hospitalized for eight days at the Cedars-Sinai Medical Center in Los Angeles for treatment of what was described as a pinched nerve and mild pneumonia. It was a harbinger of things to come, but, for the time being, it was not that serious. His spokesperson, Susan Reynolds, told an anxious press corps that 'Mr. Sinatra told me when I spoke to him that he's doing OK, he's feeling great.'

As he left the hospital after eight days, the Chairman of the Board told reporters who gathered expecting the worst: 'My doctor recommended that I go home — and I suggest the same thing for the cameras camped out at the end of my driveway . . . Seriously, though, I'm feeling better and thank everyone for their concern. It's great to be home.'

On January 9, 1997, though, fans held their breath as it was announced that Frank Sinatra had suffered a heart attack. 'He appears to have had an uncomplicated heart attack and is undergoing tests, observation and treatment, and the prognosis is good,' said Dr. Rex Kennamer. According to information released at the time by hospital spokesman Ron Wise, an uncomplicated heart attack usually means a patient doesn't need intensive care. Indeed, UCLA cardiologist Dr. Antoine Hage said that generally an 'uncomplicated heart attack' is one that does not result in significant heart failure or pumping dysfunction, and after eight days at Cedars-Sinai, Ol' Blue Eyes was able to go home again.

In April 1997, the Chairman of the Board received the ultimate tribute. President Clinton signed the legislation to award Frank Sinatra a Congressional Gold Medal. The House had cleared the bill authorizing the issuance of the award on a voice vote, and the Senate had passed the legislation in February.

This prestigious honor recognized Sinatra's accomplishments as a singer and actor

and his humanitarian activities. New York Democrat Jose Serrano, the chief sponsor of the bill, said the medal is 'my way of saying thank you to this individual who brought so much joy to the world with his talent.'

Congress had previously approved 125 gold medals for prominent Americans including entertainers such as Bob Hope, John Wayne and Danny Thomas. Serrano's press secretary said Nancy Sinatra described her father as being 'in tears' after the bill passed.

When it was announced that the image on the medallion would be a young, bow-tied Sinatra, Serrano, who had said that he preferred the felt hat and trench coat of the 1950s, reportedly commented 'The "Pal Joey" image, that says it all.'

In December 1997, Frank Sinatra would celebrate his eighty-second birthday. At Joseph 'Sparky' Spaccavento's Piccolo's restaurant in Hoboken, New Jersey, more than 500 friends and long-time fans gathered to toast Ol' Blue Eyes in the town where it all had started. There wasn't a dry eye in the place as they recalled his immortal song, 'I'm From New Jersey.'

The Chairman of the Board was well enough to attend the annual Frank Sinatra Celebrity Golf Tournament held on Friday, February 6 and Saturday, February 7, 1998 at Westin Mission Hills Resort in Rancho Mirage.

On hand for this moment and to celebrate the tenth anniversary of the tournament, were such veteran actors as Clint East- wood, Jack Lemmon, Robert Wagner, Dennis Franz, and Joe Pesci. These celebrity golfers joined others from around he world, who came to be with Frank Sinatra and to help raise money for the Barbara Sinatra Children's Center at the Eisenhower Medical Center and Palm Springs' Desert Hospital. The headliner at the 1998 event, which was officially presented by Firstplus Financial of Texas, was singer Kenny Rogers.

There's no doubting Francis Albert Sinatra's position in history. One of the greatest of popular performers, the entertainment world is a better place for his contributions, which guarantee him the immortality only a recording artist can enjoy. What makes his songs so special? The legendary sportscaster Howard Cosell, summed it up brilliantly: 'Frank Sinatra, who has the phrasing, who has the control, who understands the composers, who knows what losing means as so many have, who made the great comeback, who stands still, enduringly, on top of the entertainment world. Ladies and gentlemen, from here on in it's Frank Sinatra!'

Perhaps one of the most lasting tributes to his talent came from Rosemary Clooney, who recorded one of her first records at Columbia with him. 'He's the singer of our century, he's the one who set the standard, he's the benchmark that we have to try to reach,' she said. 'Working with him was a wonderful experience.'

Ol' Blue Eyes will live forever through his music.

Above: Frank Sinatra talks with Larry King during a live broadcast from the Cable New Network (CNN) studios in Washington, DC on May 29, 1988. The photo is courtesy of UPI.

FRANCIS ALBERT SINATRA
'The singer of our century'

*December 12, 1915 – May 14, 1998*